R.K. PACHAURI

A Global Shift to Gandhi

Earth-Shastra and Humane Arthashastra

Contributors
Dr. Saroj Pachauri
Dr. Rashmi Pachauri Rajan
Dr. Shonali Pachauri
Dr. Ash Pachauri
Anoop Variyambath
Ravi Nair
Remigius Fernandes

Cover Design
Harun Ahmed

First edition

Contents

Foreword

It is both an honor and a solemn duty to pen this foreword for *A Global Shift to Gandhi: Earth-Shastra and Humane Arthashastra*, a book that captures the essence of my dear friend and fellow Nobel Peace Prize laureate, Dr. R.K. Pachauri. Dr. Pachauri was a towering figure in the global fight against climate change and a man of deep conviction, guided by principles of equity, justice, and compassion. His passing on February 13, 2020, was a profound loss to the world, but his spirit lives on through his work, words, and unwavering commitment to a better future for all.

In this book, Dr. Pachauri offers a powerful, urgent, and timeless message to humanity. He draws inspiration from the life and philosophy of Mahatma Gandhi, a leader who, like Dr. Pachauri, understood that true progress must be measured not by material wealth but by the wellbeing of the most vulnerable among us. Gandhi's ideals of simplicity, non-violence, and social justice are not just historical footnotes but guiding beacons in our current struggle with the twin crises of environmental degradation and growing inequality.

Dr. Pachauri's concept of *Earth-Shastra* is a call to realign our relationship with nature. It challenges us to rethink the foundations of our economic and social systems, placing the Earth at the heart of all our endeavors. It reminds us that we are not separate from the natural world but deeply intertwined with it and that humanity's survival is not just a matter of choice but a necessity that depends on our ability to live in harmony with the planet that sustains us.

In *Humane Arthashastra*, Dr. Pachauri redefines the concept of wealth and prosperity. He envisions a world where economic systems are not driven by greed and exploitation but by compassion, equity, and a sense of shared responsibility. This vision resonates deeply with my own beliefs, forged through decades of struggle for the rights and dignity of my people. Like Dr. Pachauri, I have seen firsthand the devastating impact of inequality and environmental degradation on the most vulnerable communities. I share his conviction that a just and sustainable world is not only possible but imperative.

Throughout his life, Dr. Pachauri was a tireless advocate for those who often lacked a voice in global discussions—those living in poverty, marginalized communities, and future generations. His work with the Intergovernmental Panel on Climate Change (IPCC) brought the urgency of climate action to the world's attention, and his leadership inspired countless individuals and organizations to join the fight for a more equitable and sustainable future.

This book is a testament to Dr. Pachauri's legacy. It is a call to action for all of us to embrace the values that guided his life and work—values I resound with at the core, rooted in justice, equity, and a deep respect for the Earth. As we face the challenges of our time, let us draw strength from his words and vision. Let us honor his memory by committing ourselves to the path he has laid out, which leads to the preservation of our planet and the creation of a more just and compassionate world.

Dr. Pachauri was not just a friend; he was a fighter for the planet and the future of humanity. His legacy is a beacon of hope in these challenging times, and I am proud to lend my voice to his message. May this book inspire a global shift in consciousness, reflecting the wisdom of Gandhi and the unyielding spirit of Dr. Pachauri.

With deep respect and solidarity,

J. Ramos-Horta
Nobel Peace Prize Laureate (1996)
President of Timor-Leste (2022-2027), (2007-2012)

Foreword

I am thrilled and deeply honored to add my voice and words as a foreword to this marvelous book. In his song "Glory" the recording artist John Legend tells of the "wisdom of the elders, the young people's energy." Ingredients of both of these are required to bring about deep and meaningful social change. I heard these words sung in a new way when Mr. Legend headlined the Nobel Peace Prize concert in Oslo in 2017, in honor of the International Campaign to Abolish Nuclear Weapons (ICAN), the 2017 Nobel Peace Prize winner, a campaign I helped to start in 2007.

John Legend's respect for both elders and youth is encapsulated never better than in this glorious work by the late but timelessly remembered Dr. R.K Pachauri. As I read this manuscript, I felt myself in conversation with one of our most helpful elders in the movement to protect our beautiful planet. And he points the way, with articulate, careful, passionate scholarship, to another elder, the great Mahatma Gandhi.

But he doesn't stop there. No, he honors the young people's energy, insight, and integrity. He pays specific tribute to Greta Thunberg. And it is clear, through this, his last manuscript, and through the POP Movement, which, along with Dr. Ash Pachauri, is his last great gathering of the next generation, that he had a deep belief in the future, a future filled with hope and harmony, integrity, compassion and connection.

Dr. Pachauri was honored in 2007 when the Intergovernmental Panel on Climate Change, which he led, was awarded the Nobel Peace Prize. The greatest honor we can bestow on him now is to heed his words.

At present, we find ourselves in grave danger due to the twin existential threats of the climate crisis and the ongoing, escalating presence of nuclear weapons. Given our predicament, a radical solution is sorely needed. Gandhi provided us with a set of choices, and Dr. Pachauri has shown us that they apply to our current crises. So the question is this: Will we have the courage to lead into a sustainable and hopeful future?

In hope and determination,

Dr. Ruth A. Mitchell
Neurosurgeon
Chair of the Board, International Physicians for the Prevention of Nuclear War (IPPNW) (Nobel Peace Prize 1985)
Former Chair of the Board, International Campaign to Abolish Nuclear Weapons (ICAN) Australia (Nobel Peace Prize 2017)

Preface

Human society is now looking increasingly at where our civilization has gone wrong and what needs to be done to change the pattern of what we have been given to accept as the path of growth and development for enhancing human welfare. Scientists, political leaders, and ordinary citizens are finding compelling evidence on how the human condition itself is deteriorating and undergoing continuous and rapid degradation. At the same time, the assets which nature has bestowed on us are in a state of alarming and perpetual decline. Over the past three decades, consciousness about human induced climate change and the risks it is imposing through its growing impacts, have entered our consciousness on a collective and continuing basis.

The fact that something is wrong with our pattern of development and the global agreements that we have in place is brought out by the fact that, for instance, the United Nations Framework Convention on Climate Change (UNFCCC) has been in existence for over a quarter century, but emissions of greenhouse gases increased in 2018 in clear neglect of the very objectives of the UNFCCC. Many voices are now being raised on the impossibility of bringing the ecosystems of this planet back to a reasonably healthy state so that the extinction of species is reduced or halted, services provided by the assets of nature and its ecosystems are revived, and the risks from climate change minimized to ensure that disasters in the future do not endanger human society and other species on planet earth. There are some who deny the trends that spell doom for this planet's ecosystems, and there is perhaps an equal number who just give up in helpless resignation and who seem to come up with the futility of solutions that humans can possibly devise as a timely answer. These persons feel a state of despair and inevitability about doom and gloom in the future. Yet, there is a rational set of individuals displaying a sense of responsibility and urgency by which they see the need for change as radically essential and inevitable. Mahatma Gandhi said, "A small body of determined spirits fired by an unquenchable faith in their mission can alter the course of history."

If we are to study the life of Gandhi, we draw inspiration from what this humble and spiritually strong human being was able to achieve in a lifetime against the mightiest empire on earth and in support of the 300 million impoverished Indians who lived at the time when Gandhi mounted his non-violent struggle for India's independence. I was a child when India attained independence, and all of us, including the large majority of adults in the country, looked at him as the incarnation of God and a transformer of society who could achieve miraculous results.

Gandhi's 150th anniversary fell on his birthday in 2019 and if he were alive today, he would have reflected on the whole history of the industrial revolution which was in full swing when he took birth. He was an individual who was driven by his inflexible and unshakable beliefs in the values that were part of his character, but he was a good learner and willing to change his views within the bounds of reason. For instance, he admitted that "machinery has its place; it has come to stay...... I am not against machinery as such. The *charkha* (hand spinning wheel) itself, for that matter, is machinery. But I am a determined foe of all machinery that is designed for exploitation of people". Perhaps, Gandhi would have been totally sensitive to mechanization that dispossesses ordinary human beings and exploits them, but perhaps he would also have seen information technology as an enabler of human beings and a supporter of their skills and higher productivity. He would, no doubt, have seen the yawning gap between the elite rich of the world, who are getting richer by the day, and the static mass of poverty, which clearly reflects the exploitation of society by a privileged few at the cost of a substantial number who see no improvement in their lives and wellbeing.

This book is a grim reminder of Gandhi's view of life which fully relates in equal measure to the grim reality of depressing statistics and parameters and which spell destruction and degradation of nature's resources and invaluable assets. More so, it looks at the directions in which the very quality of human life is moving towards an increasingly unsustainable future. It also focuses on how the youth of this world would, within a short period of time, suffer the horrible consequences of our current patterns of development which gives us un-Gandhian pleasures and values and which are myopic and transitory while at the same time affecting the very basis on which all forms of life can be sustained in the future. A Gandhian view should convince us of the drastic and radical manner in which human society needs to change with a sense of urgency. Such change will, no doubt, not be painless but it would ensure that we reach a level of comfort, stability, and security over time once the initial but temporary pain is over. Anything beyond this approach would be disastrous simply because at this stage, against the background of forces which are destroying this planet's resources and the value they provide to all species, we have no soft options.

It was in the early 1990s that my late colleague at The Energy and Resources Institute (TERI), Dr. Triloki Nath Khoshoo, a brilliant scientist and human being of the most superior kind, started studying Mahatma Gandhi's works. He found a wealth of wisdom and good sense in Gandhi's beliefs related to nature, the very purpose of human development and how Gandhian thought would become a beacon light for human society in its quest for sustainability and what it perceives as the essence of growth and development for all. I encouraged Dr. Khoshoo to publish a book on this subject, which he gave the title "Mahatma Gandhi: An Apostle of Applied Human Ecology." This precious booklet was first published in 1995, reprinted in 1996, and then again in 2002 as a tribute to Dr. T.N. Khoshoo who sadly had departed from this world. In the year 2019, Mahatma Gandhi's thinking and philosophy as apostle of applied human ecology is if anything even more compelling than it was when Dr. Khoshoo's book was first published. Hence, in a world which is currently grappling with the negative impacts and externalities imposed by human society on this planet and the resources that it provides, Gandhi's message becomes sharper and clearer. His view recommends a sharp turn in direction for what we have accepted as the established pattern of growth and development with breathtakingly rapid and drastic changes which cannot be delayed any longer.

This volume examines the risks associated with climate change and damage to the earth's ecosystems which clearly spell large-scale disaster. The Intergovernmental Panel on Climate Change (IPCC), since it is established in 1988, has brought out a series of assessment reports which clearly provide the scientific basis for human induced climate change, their increasing impacts, including extreme events that they are imposing on society across the globe. Gandhi rightly said: "A technological society has two choices. First, it can wait until catastrophic failures expose systemic deficiencies, distortion and self-deceptions... Second, a culture can provide social checks and balances to correct for systemic distortion prior to catastrophic failures."

Despite the overwhelming scientific explanation for what human activities are doing to the global commons, including the disruption of a relatively stable climate, we are now in the grips of growing self-deception. Hence, it would be appropriate to accept Gandhi's advice and provide the social checks and balances that would avoid disaster and catastrophic failures.

The remedy lies in disruptive change because there are severe limits to incremental efforts, which, at best, would make a marginal difference to the outcomes which would be in our interests collectively to achieve. Gandhi was not averse to disruptive change, whether it was the sparse clothing he wore, the simple lifestyle that he led, and the restraints he imposed on himself as a distinct and sharp change from what he had been brought up with. The world needs drastic and disruptive change which goes far beyond technological choices, minor economic and policy changes, but which emphasizes the acceptance of religion and philosophy distinctly different from what we practice today. It also requires a deliberate reduction in material wants and curbing the spread of consumerism, which has emanated from the countries of the West since the beginning of industrialization.

Gandhi examines these disruptive changes and in no way advocates a departure from capitalism, which many analysts are articulating today. He does, however, advocate a new form of capitalism which serves the fair and equitable needs of society. We also do not favor the advocacy by several ecological economists of "degrowth" policies, by which GDP growth goes down to a negative level. On the other hand, what is favored is economic growth, which takes into account the negative externalities and the reduction of nature's wealth and the ecosystem services that human society and all living species benefit from and, indeed, survive on. All in all, with the growing clamor for bringing about change, which may just about help our planet to barely survive, the Gandhian way of life is an extremely effective and sustainable goal for human society to reach. Anything more selfish and efforts that ignore the enormous loss of biodiversity and the earth's ecosystems would ultimately lead to major hazards being faced by human beings as well. While Gandhi's views and values may appear radical and perhaps even impossible to consider seriously, his approach seems the most appropriate and worthy of deep reflection and application. As evidence of our path of development, which relies on increasingly unsustainable consumption and production, Gandhi provides us with a set of choices which while difficult, given our current values and mental inertia, appear to be the most attractive hopes for the future.

Prelude

*Introduction to A Global Shift to Gandhi: Earth-Shastra and
Humane Arthashastra by Dr. R.K. Pachauri*

Dr. R.K. Pachauri, a visionary leader and global advocate for sustainable development, spent his life championing the cause of environmental preservation and social equity. His profound understanding of the interconnectedness of humanity and nature inspired him to write this book, *A Global Shift to Gandhi: Earth-Shastra and Humane Arthashastra*.

Tragically, Dr. Pachauri passed away on February 13, 2020, before he could see this important work come to fruition. In honor of his enduring legacy, his family has taken the responsibility to publish this book, recognizing that its message is more vital today than ever.

This book is not just a reflection of Dr. Pachauri's deep reverence for Mahatma Gandhi's principles but also a clarion call to the world—a blueprint for realigning our path toward a sustainable and equitable future. As we stand at the precipice of environmental catastrophe, the lessons encapsulated within these pages offer a guiding light, reminding us that the wisdom of the past can pave the way for a better tomorrow.

Earth-Shastra *and* ***Humane Arthashastra*** are the cornerstones of this book's philosophy. Derived from the ancient Indian concepts of governance and statecraft, Dr. Pachauri reinterprets these terms to align with Gandhi's vision of a just and sustainable society.

Earth-Shastra represents a holistic approach to development that places the Earth—the source of all life—at the center of human endeavors. It calls for a deep respect for nature's limits and an understanding that true progress cannot come at the expense of environmental degradation. In this framework, the Earth is not merely a resource to be exploited but a living entity to be nurtured and protected.

Humane Arthashastra, on the other hand, reimagines the traditional concept of wealth and prosperity. Drawing from Gandhi's teachings, it advocates for a form of compassionate and just capitalism, where economic activities are conducted with the wellbeing of all members of society in mind. It challenges the current paradigm of unchecked consumerism and inequality, urging us to pursue a path of equitable, inclusive, and sustainable development.

Together, these concepts encapsulate the essence of Gandhi's philosophy—one that seeks harmony between human aspirations and the natural world and between material wealth and spiritual wellbeing. Dr. Pachauri's message to the world through this book is clear: We must urgently shift our mindset and actions toward a development model that respects our planet's finite resources and upholds the dignity and wellbeing of all its inhabitants.

As you embark on this journey through the pages of *A Global Shift to Gandhi*, may you be inspired by Dr. Pachauri's vision and empowered to contribute to the global movement for a more sustainable and just world—a world that honors the legacy of both Mahatma Gandhi and Dr. R.K. Pachauri.

Speed is Irrelevant if You are Going in the Wrong Direction

There are several aspects of Gandhi's thought which have relevance to solving the catastrophic trends that we see in evidence today. His belief was to focus on a person's immediate surroundings to the exclusion of the more remote. Indeed, this is a principle on which an intimate relationship had developed over time where human beings accepted responsibility for the natural resources around them. That was clearly the arrangement which existed in India before the British imposed colonialism on the country. With a desire to source a large volume of timber products, which was produced in profusion across the length and breadth of India, the colonial power nationalized forests on the plea that local communities were patently irresponsible and would rapidly destroy forest resources. This gave the British an opportunity to exploit and ship precious timber, such as the best quality teak, to the UK for the construction of railway coaches, ships, furniture, buildings, and many products. Local communities were, therefore, dispossessed and, indeed, to fulfill their own needs took resort to illegal felling of trees to some extent in contrast with the almost religious manner in which they looked after them earlier on a sustainable basis.

Gandhi was also very conscious of his ideal of economic equality. His belief was that the rich must function as trustees of the wealth they possessed, which, in his view, was held on behalf of the poor. He felt that wealth held in trust for the poor would make expropriation by legislative enactment unnecessary. His belief in democracy was essentially based on a stateless democracy consisting of a federation of village communities functioning on the basis of voluntary cooperation and dignified and peaceful co-existence. To this extent, his model came very close to that of a cooperative. The success of cooperatives in different parts of the world has generally ensured equality of opportunities, fair and equitable distribution of income, growing wealth, and aggregate prosperity for any such enterprise. In India itself, the so-called white revolution spearheaded by Dr. Verghese Kurien, wherein milk production through the cooperative system was 55.8 million tonnes with an availability of 178 gms/day per capita in 1991-92 reached 176.3 million tonnes with availability of 375 gms/day per capita in 2017-18. This dramatic increase took place from a totally deficient and stagnant level before the introduction of cooperatives. Other regions, however, have also attained similar success given the right conditions.

In the year 1935, Gandhi expressed the view, "I look upon an increase in the power of the State with the greatest fear because although while apparently doing good by minimizing exploitation, it does the greatest harm to mankind by destroying individuality which lies at the heart of all progress." Perhaps this view also relates to the warning issued by General Eisenhower when he was laying down office as the US President and when he warned about the power of the "military-industrial complex." In today's world, the enormous resources and powers that vested interests are able to muster and control distort the very objectives of democratic governments elected for the good of society by the voters belonging to that society. Wars are often started by those who are in the business of production of arms and earning huge profits. The health of human beings is severely ruined by those who are in the business of producing and selling tobacco products.

Human induced climate change is becoming progressively severe because those earning large scale profits from fossil fuels delay retard the introduction of lower carbon substitutes to replace them. What they find convenient is to continue with their easy profits even though the externalities associated with concentration of carbon dioxide in the atmosphere take the form of human induced climate change with all its impacts and growing risks. It is also well known that the lobbies representing some of these industries use their money and power to muffle the voices of those who provide a rational basis for change. This author has been the subject of underhand efforts and outright dissemination of false information in an attempt to see that the science of climate change cannot be spread to the general public and decision makers. After the Fourth Assessment Report (AR4) of the IPCC was released and in the wake of the Nobel Peace Prize, which this author received on behalf of the IPCC, a large scale campaign was mounted by climate skeptics and the fossil fuel lobby to discredit the findings of the AR4. Such attempts have continued over the past ten years and indeed they have been partly effective in sowing doubts in the minds of decision makers and public at large. It took a young 16-year old Swedish girl Greta Thunberg to mobilize public opinion in 2019 to be able to sensitize world leaders to the dangers and immorality of climate change based on an obsession with continuation of our consumerist tendencies.

An article in The Guardian asks the question, "Ending climate change requires the end of capitalism. Have we got the stomach for it?" The article begins by saying, "Policy tweaks won't do it. We need to throw the kitchen sink at this with a total rethink of our relationship to ownership, work, and capital". Several people across the world now believe that the way economic progress has been defined has led to a malaise which is causing huge negative impacts on the welfare of human society. If we take the case of growing inequalities, the Oxfam report published in early 2019 comes up with the startling finding that the world's billionaires are growing $2.5 billion richer every day, while the poorest half of the global population is seeing its net worth dwindle. Billionaires who in 2019 numbered a record of 2,208 have more wealth than ever before according to the 2019 Oxfam International report. Shockingly, the combined fortunes of the world's 26 richest individuals reached $1.4 trillion last year which represents the same amount as the total wealth of 3.8 billion poorest people. This certainly does not represent the philosophy of Gandhi, who believed that the rich are trustees of the wealth they own essentially on behalf of society as a whole. Gandhi was critical of the pattern of economic growth and development pursued by the countries of the world. This pattern was based on the concept of economies of scale with large scale centralization of production and manufacturing facilities which led to rapid urbanization. The result is that today, every country in the world, both developed and developing, follows a monoculture of development based on rapid urbanization.

Urban centers have been there since time immemorial but they were hardly seen as locations to which people from rural areas flocked to seek employment and live without any basic infrastructure or services, often in slums which are totally uninhabitable. In the earliest examples of urbanization, typically, the poorest people lived on the periphery, while the more affluent sections of society lived in the city center.

It was by the middle of the 18th century, with the advent of the industrial revolution, that older cities were transformed into newer systems. This generally resulted in factories and manufacturing facilities being located on the outskirts of the cities and other commercial establishments, including banking, trading units, and other enterprises of a commercial nature, occupying spaces in the downtown areas of cities. By the end of the 19th century, several cities in Western Europe and America expanded their population in urban locations beyond 30% of the total. At the same time, for the working class, housing was provided on the outskirts of cities close to the factories which provided employment. Technological developments related to transportation systems such as trains, trams, and automobiles led to rapid growth of cities and with the provision of lifts and elevators the heights of buildings also increased. Since income levels in developing countries remain generally low, the provision of basic infrastructure and services for the benefit of the poor remains heavily underfunded, and, therefore, the larger cities in the developing world are taken up by slums, which often accommodate 40% or more of city dwellers who have migrated from rural locations. Yet, the expansion of employment opportunities, which are generally absent in rural locations, attracts millions of city dwellers in search of jobs and livelihoods, even in the absence of very basic services in shanty towns. That these trends are likely to compound the problems of the future was something that Gandhi understood and foresaw as an inferior form of urbanization and which emulated trends in the developed countries.

There are several other implications and effects of the Western model of growth and development. These include a massive reduction in nature's wealth and natural assets which not only serve human society but living species of all forms. World Wildlife Fund (WWF) publishes every two years its Living Planet Report and in the 2018 version, it states, "On average, we've seen an astonishing 60% decline in the size of populations of mammals, birds, fish, reptiles, and amphibians in just over 40 years. The top threats to species identified in the report link directly to human activities, including habitat loss and degradation and the excessive use of wildlife such as overfishing and overhunting." At the same time, the earth is estimated to have lost about half of its shallow water corals in the past 30 years; a fifth of the Amazon forests has disappeared in just 50 years. The WWF also estimated that on a global basis, nature provides services worth around US$125 trillion a year while also helping supply fresh air, clean water, food, energy, medicines, and much more. Essentially, therefore, what we measure as the increase in the GDP represents a massive decline in both the wealth that this planet holds for the benefit of all and the services it provides for human society and all living species. We explore the flaws of GDP as a measure of human progress in later pages, which only brings to the surface the criticism that

Gandhi repeatedly highlighted with the Western model of democracy and development. Democracy and the practice of capitalism, as seen across various countries of the developed world, have, to a large extent, been hijacked by vested interests.

The issue to be considered is how the current trends spreading across every society reflect human values which are being eroded through a universally uniform monoculture and whether such development can be reversed in a steady and smooth manner. The answer to this question would be a resounding "no" because there may be merit in a drastic and disruptive change that goes to the very heart of the system that we see prevailing worldwide, and certainly, no such process would work by which rapid progress can be made through steady trends. A tectonic shift is the only solution. We need to take a global view in a world that is shrinking every day.

Africa is currently home to almost 1.3 billion people but it is expected that by 2050 this figure would reach 2.5 billion. With a large number of people living in poverty and a low level of literacy and education, the prospects of decline in fertility do not appear very bright. For instance, from the 1950s, fertility of that continent rose slightly, reaching seven children per woman by the early 1970s. However, following that period, there was a sharp divergence in different regions. In northern and southern Africa, fertility rates declined. In northern Africa, for instance, fertility reduced from seven children per woman in the 1960s to five by the late 1980s and then to three by 2005 – 2010. In southern Africa, where fertility rates were six children per woman in the 1960s, the level dropped to four in the late 1980s and down to 2.71 in 2005-2010. In the case of eastern Africa, however, fertility rates remained above seven children per woman even in the late 1980s. This then declined to remain at nearly five in 2010-2015.

The essential point that needs to be emphasized is to stress that the pattern of urbanization followed in the West cannot possibly be emulated on a continent like Africa where the large majority of the population still lives away from towns and cities. If Gandhian principles of economic development were to be respected, they clearly have huge relevance to Africa. If we do not follow the approach of treating non-urban areas as the focus of development, there would be enormous exploitation of one group over another leading to growing conflict and widespread violence. To a large extent, Africa is still being subjected to colonial attitudes because even though the continent has a large volume of minerals and hydrocarbon resources, it is essentially the corporate organizations from the developed world which reap all the benefits from exploitation of these resources. It is tragic that all the surpluses generated by these corporations benefit only the shareholders and the powerful in the developed world, with little investments being made in the countries which export these commodities.

There is perhaps a need for an international convention that clearly provides a curb on some of these unhealthy practices along with the development of alternative models emphasizing non-urban development as a much higher priority than the provision of infrastructure, resources, and human capacity in urban locations.

Gandhi was particularly sensitive to one class of human beings exploiting others who are not fortunate enough to possess the same means and those whose wealth and income leave them few options but to be subservient to the exploiters. He regarded this form of economic exploitation as a severe case of violence, which clearly meant that he was extending the concept of violence to unfair or unjustified exploitation of those who could be regarded as weaker in terms of social status, wealth, and income than the exploiters. Gandhi believed:

There are times when you have to obey a call which is the highest of all, i.e., the voice of conscience even though such obedience may cost many a bitter tear, and even more separation from friends, from family, from the state to which you may belong, from all you have held as dear as life itself. For this obedience is the law of our being.... To deprive a man of his natural liberty and to deny to him the ordinary amenities of life is worse than starving the body, it is starvation of the soul, the dweller in the body.

This, of course, was his view on colonial rule but it applied equally to slavery, the scourge of apartheid on South Africa, and denial of civil rights in particular. He was, therefore, critical of American and European ways of life which had historically and even today denied natural liberty to so many.

The incessant search for material comforts and their multiplication is an evil. I make bold to say that the Europeans will have to remodel their outlook, if they are not to perish under the weight of the comforts to which they are becoming slaves.

He warned the Western world of the grim scenario that lay ahead.

A time is coming when those who are in the mad rush today of multiplying their wants will retrace their steps and say; what have we done.... Modern civilization is such that one has only to be patient and it will be self-destroyed.

At the beginning of the 20th century, many Western societies exploited other societies, such as in the case of colonialism. This obviously had an acute impact on Gandhi's thinking, who saw this form of violence as part of a historical process. Clearly, US society, as it exists today, conquered their vast territories by first decimating Indigenous tribes and then through the migration of slaves from the African continent to provide labor for economic activities under extremely inhuman conditions. They also waged war on their neighbors, such as Mexico, annexing large areas of land as their own territory. Gandhi apparently related even some of the flaws in US society today with the historical atrocities that he felt were an inherent part of the so called economic progress of that society. Similarly, the efforts by the UK to impose its will and inequitable form of government through colonialism possibly defined the nature and behavior of that country towards the rest of the developing world. The UK was also a major factor in slavery in various parts of the world.

Gandhi saw today's practice of democracy as a reflection of the historical developments of the past which were characterized by the exploitation of one class by another. It was for this reason that he abhorred transplantation of governments from western societies to a developing country like India. His warnings on this account were unheeded and today, even in the developing countries, we see trends similar to those in western societies, resulting in the wealthiest minority becoming wealthier and the status of the poor remaining essentially unchanged, leading to major disparities in wealth and income. Gandhi saw this as an extension of violence which he fought for all his life through non-violent means.

The UN University has come up with a very interesting viewpoint on whether rural populations have greater resilience than those in urban areas. In a paper published essentially on this issue with the title "Return to Rural Communities: Resilience over Efficiency", it looks at the example of a family that moved from Zurich in Switzerland to a village deep in the Alps of Switzerland and it describes the life that this family followed in the Zurich location vs. what they were able to benefit from in the rural area which they moved to. The interesting point of view put forward in this paper is that perhaps specialization is antithetical to resilience. What this publication suggests is that in urban locations where there is a whole range of specializations, this clearly provides for very narrow skills on the part of the population in these locations; these do not make the inhabitants resilient.

What this publication puts forward is the fact that efficiency is one of the keys to economic growth. However, such efficiency is often achieved through increased specialization and the fact that many urban residents have a small range of highly specialized skills such as accounting, legal advising, pediatrics, etc., and, of course, they exercise these skills in an efficient way. Further, they rely on other specialists to meet the fundamental needs of their daily existence and their daily lives. However, if we look at rural locations, we find that there is much greater resilience, and the publication refers to a Robinson Crusoe type economy where one single individual, viz. Robinson Crusoe is responsible for every single task that he carries out on his island. This view also accords with what has been brought out by the Intergovernmental Science-Policy Platform on Biodiversity and Ecosystem Services (IPBES) in its report, wherein Indigenous communities are regarded as being far more effective in managing the natural resources around them than those who have no knowledge of these indigenous skills and traditions.

In an age when climate change and other natural disasters are going to increase in both frequency and intensity, it is necessary to build resilience within communities, and these essentially would be based on a rural system of development than urban centers, which according to the UNU paper is essentially based on specialized skills, and these skills do not necessarily cut across their narrow specializations to build the integrated approach to resilience that is a function of a more general and a broader set of skills that rural populations embody. Since the trend in urbanization essentially started in Europe, notwithstanding ancient cities like Mohenjo-Daro and Harappa and the others in the Middle East, the rapid rate of urbanization in both developing and developed countries merits some reflection. Large cities across the globe essentially display a uniform culture, and the breakdown of the family structure leading to nuclear families.

It is also a well known principle in economies that the marginal propensity to consume (MPC) is much higher at lower income levels. In China, as also in India, boosting rural incomes would help in creating a much larger extent of demand for goods and services. China still has 40% of its population in rural areas. A recent report by the Beijing Orient Agribusiness Consultant states that rural income in China has been on the decline since 2014 and dropped by another 20% in the first half of 2019. This is clearly the result of China's policies of promoting urban development through infrastructure developments in towns and cities.

Ecological Movement Designed to Prevent Violence Against Nature

The Intergovernmental Science-Policy Platform on Biodiversity and Ecosystem Services (IPBES) has, in its 2019 report, brought out some startling facts, which clearly show that the earth is being subjected to stresses that are far in excess of the carrying capacity of ecosystems and related natural systems. For instance, 75% of the land surface has been significantly altered, 66% of the ocean area is experiencing increasing cumulative impacts, and over 85% of wetlands in terms of area have been lost. While the rate of forest loss has slowed globally since 2000, this is distributed unequally. Most disturbing is the recent burning of the Amazon rainforests in Brazil and several other parts of Latin America. Across much of the tropics which have a high level of biodiversity, 32 million hectares of primary or recovering forests were lost between 2010 and 2015. This may be accompanied by tropical and subtropical forests increasing within some countries and the global extent of temperate and boreal forests actually increasing. However, a range of actions, from restoration of natural forests to planting of monocultures, contribute to these increases and have very different consequences for biodiversity and its contributions as a service to people and other species.

Approximately half of the live coral cover on coral reefs has been lost since the 1870s while accelerating losses in recent decades due to climate change end up exacerbating other drivers. The average and normal abundance of nature's species in most major terrestrial biomes has fallen by at least 20%, thus potentially affecting ecosystem processes and, hence, nature's contributions to people and other species. This decline has taken place mostly since 1900 but may be accelerating over time. In areas of high endemism, native biodiversity has often been severely impacted by alien species of the invasive variety. Population sizes of wild water bred species have tended to decline over the last 50 years on land in fresh water, and in the sea. Global trends in insect populations are not known but rapid declines have been well documented in some places. An average of around 25% of species in assessed animal and plant groups are threatened. This suggests that around one million species already face extinction, many within decades, unless action is taken to reduce the intensity of biodiversity loss. Without such action, there will be a further acceleration in the global rate of species extinction which is already at least tens to hundreds of times higher than it has been averaged over the past 10 million years.

The rate of global change in nature during the past 50 years is unprecedented in human history. The total drivers of change in nature, with the largest global impact, have been changes in land and sea use, which have the most serious impacts, direct exploitation of organisms, climate change, pollution, and invasion of alien species. These five direct drivers result from an array of underlying causes, the indirect drivers of change, which are, in turn, underpinned by societal values and behavior that include production and consumption patterns, human population dynamics and trends, trade, technological innovations, and local through global governance. The rate of change in the direct and indirect drivers differs among regions and countries.

Past and ongoing rapid declines in biodiversity, ecosystem services and functions, and many of nature's contributions to people and other species mean that most established societal and environmental goals, such as goals embodied in the Aichi Biodiversity Targets and the 2030 Agenda for Sustainable Development, will not be achieved based on current trajectories. These declines will also undermine other goals, such as those specified in the Paris Agreement adopted under the United Nations Frame Convention on Climate Change and the 2050 Vision for Biodiversity. The negative trends in biodiversity and ecosystem functions are projected to continue or worsen in many future scenarios in response to indirect drivers such as rapid human population growth, unsustainable production and consumption, and associated technological development. In sharp contrast, scenarios and pathways that explore the effects of low to moderate population growth and transformative changes in the production and consumption of energy, food, feed material, fiber, and water, Sustainable use, and equitable sharing of the benefits arising from use in nature friendly climate adaption and mitigation will better support the achievement of future societal and environmental objectives.

Areas of the world projected to experience significant negative effects from global changes in climate, biodiversity, ecosystem functions and services, and nature's contributions to people and other species are also home to large concentrations of Indigenous peoples and many of the world's poorest communities. Except in scenarios that include transformative change, negative trends in nature, ecosystem functions, and many of nature's contributions to people are projected to continue to 2050 and beyond due to the projected impacts of increasing land/sea use change, exploitation of organisms, and climate change.

Societal goals, including those for food, water, energy, health, the achievement of human wellbeing for all, mitigating and adapting to climate change, and conserving and sustainably using nature, can be achieved in sustainable pathways through the rapid and improved deployment of the existing policy instruments and new initiatives that more effectively enlist individual and collective action for transformative change. Hence, we have reached a stage in the degradation and destruction of ecosystem services and the wealth of nature which clearly requires transformative change to bring about a restoration of what would perhaps be considered as moving towards a healthy state with these assets. Transformative change in its ideal form involves a rapid shift to Gandhian philosophy which would also provide human beings greater happiness, wellbeing, and satisfaction.

Specifically, the following changes are mutually reinforcing:

1. Enabling visions of a good quality of lives that do not entail ever increasing material consumption.
2. Lowering total consumption and waste including by addressing both population and GDP-related growth and per capita consumption differently in different contexts.
3. Unleashing existing widely held values of responsibility to affect new social norms for sustainability, especially by adopting notions of responsibility to include impacts associated with consumption, for addressing inequalities, especially regarding income and gender, which undermine the capacity for sustainability.
4. Ensuring inclusive decision making, fair and equitable sharing of benefits arising from the use of and adherence to human rights in conservation decisions.
5. Accounting for nature deterioration from local economic activities and socioeconomic environmental interactions over distances, including, for example, international trade, ensuring environmentally friendly technological and social innovation taking into account potential rebound effects in investment regimes.
6. Promoting education, knowledge generation, and maintenance of different knowledge systems, including the sciences and indigenous and local knowledge regarding nature, conservation, and its sustainable use.

All of these are at the very core of Gandhian thought and philosophy.

The WWF, which brings out every two years the Living Planet Report referred to earlier, has described in its latest report of 2018 that scenarios and models can help scientists visualize and explore how alternative actions affect the dynamic interdependencies between nature, nature's benefits to people, and quality of life. However, the challenge, according to WWF, is that we face not only the need to identify potential pathways that will allow us to restore biodiversity but we would also need to achieve the necessary transformation while feeding a growing population under the accelerated effects of climate change in a world which is changing rapidly. In this context, it would be useful to discuss the report of the IPCC brought out in 2019 on Climate Change and Land. This report clearly brings out the unsustainability of current patterns of food systems and diets for an ever-expanding population and, therefore, the scientific assessment clearly shows that human society will have to use plant-based diets urgently over a period of time if we have to ensure that land does not get degraded and reaches a level which is unsustainable.

The IPCC Special Report on Climate Change and Land has clearly stated, "25-30% of total GHG emissions are attributable to the food system. These are from agriculture and land use, storage, transport, packaging, processing, retail, and consumption."

Consumption of healthy and sustainable diets presents major opportunities for reducing GHG emissions from food systems and improving health outcomes.

Agriculture and the food system are key to global climate change responses. Combining supply side actions such as efficient production, transport, and processing with demand-side interventions such as modification of food choices, and reduction of food loss and waste, reduces GHG emissions and enhances food system resilience.

Figure 1

Technical mitigation potential of changing diets by 2050 according to a range of scenarios examined in the literature. Estimates are technical potential only, and include additional effects of carbon sequestration from land-sparing. Data without error bars are from one study only.

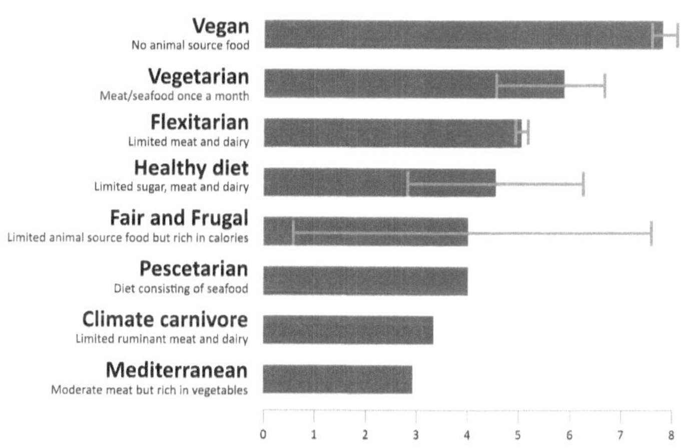

Source: IPCC Special Report on Climate Change and Land

Gandhi was a vegetarian, and he was known to repeat what George Bernard

Shaw had written in his poem "We are the living graves of murdered beasts," which is provided below:

We are the living graves of murdered beasts,
Slaughtered to satisfy our appetites.
We never pause to wonder at our feasts,
If animals, like men, can possibly have rights.

We pray on Sundays that we may have light,
To guide our footsteps on the path we tread.
We're sick of War, we do not want to fight –
The thought of it now fills our hearts with dread,

And yet – we gorge ourselves upon the dead.
Like carrion crows, we live and feed on meat,
Regardless of the suffering and pain
We cause by doing so, if thus we treat
Defenseless animals for sport or gain,
How can we hope in this world to attain
The PEACE we say we are so anxious for.

We pray for it, o'er hecatombs of slain,
To God while outraging the moral law.
Thus, cruelty begets its offspring – WAR.

Gandhi was obviously inspired by this poem because it accorded with his view that violence cannot be contained if we slaughter animals. He was a vegetarian all his life.

Of course, Gandhi was not a vegan and consumed milk, milk products, and honey. He stated, "I am a puritan myself, but I am Catholic towards others." He believed, "As long as Man continues to be the ruthless destroyer of lower living beings, he will never know health or peace. For as long as men massacre animals, they will kill each other. Indeed, he who sows the seed of murder and pain cannot reap joy and love."

On another occasion, Gandhi stated, "A human being has no power to create life. He has, therefore, no right to destroy life."

He also stated, "A society can be judged by the way it treats its animals." He saw a divine order in the universe in which all species had rights and privileges which were expressed in this quote.

In his own way, he saw the value of all the assets that nature provides, including the value of biodiversity.

He said that "There is an orderliness in the universe. There is an unalterable law governing everything and every being that exists or lives. It is no blind law; for no blind law can govern the conduct of living beings"

It is also essential to understand from the work of the IPBES and scientists working in the field that flowering plants are pollinated by insects and other animals. In fact, it has been estimated that the proportion of animal pollinated wild plant species rises from an average of 78% in the temperatezone communities to 94% in tropical communities. Pollinators are a diverse group including more than 20,000 species of insects, many other types of insects (such as flies, butterflies, moths, and beetles) and even vertebrates such as some birds and bats. Most pollinators are wild but a few species of bees can be managed such as honeybees. Our food production depends heavily on these pollinators because more than 75% of the leading global food crops benefit from pollination. Some of these crops, especially fruits and vegetables, are key sources of human nutrition.

High yields in large-scale intensive production of crops such as apples, almonds, and oilseeds depend on insect pollination. But so do the crops of small farmers in the developing world, where healthy populations of wild pollinators increase yields significantly. Economically, pollination increases the global value of crop production by anywhere from US$ 235 to 577 billion per year to growers alone. This keeps prices down for consumers by ensuring stable supplies. Changing land use due to agriculture, intense irrigation, and urban expansion is one of a number of key drivers of pollinator loss, especially when natural areas that provide breeding and nesting resources are degraded or disappear. Improving habitat diversity within the landscape and the inclusion of non-agricultural habitats within land management plans have been shown to ameliorate pollinator loss, boost pollinator numbers, and improve ecosystem services.

Another important factor which characterizes today's society across the globe is the fact that disparities within nations and across nations are growing very rapidly. It brings out the stark difference between the small number of rich people in the world and a large number of those who live in absolute poverty. The Oxfam report of 2019, for instance, clearly says that the world's billionaires have found recent years as a period of boom because since the financial crisis that shook our world and caused enormous suffering, the fortunes of the rich have risen dramatically. In the ten years since the financial crisis, the number of billionaires has nearly doubled. As stated earlier, the wealth of the world's billionaires increased by $ 900 billion in the last year (2018) alone, or at the rate of $ 2.5 billion a day. Meanwhile, the wealth of the poorest half of humanity, that is 3.8 billion people, fell by 11%. Billionaires now have more wealth than ever before. Between 2017 and 2018, a new billionaire was created every two days, and wealth is becoming even more concentrated. Last year, 26 people owned the same wealth as the 3.8 billion people who make up the poorest half of humanity, down from 43 people a year before. The world's richest man, Jeff Bezos, owner of Amazon, saw his fortune increase to $112 billion. Just 1% of his fortune is the equivalent to the whole health budget for Ethiopia, a country of 105 million people.

Several organizations have studied the state of the oceans and the extent of pollution that is destroying the major surface of the earth because oceans constitute 70% of the total surface of the earth. Most importantly, they also contain the largest resource in terms of biodiversity and largest number of species which are likely to be threatened and would get extinct with the level of pollution that human society is imposing on the oceans. One major effect of climate change is the warming of the oceans. In fact, the Fifth Assessment Report of the IPCC estimated that between 1971 and 2010, 90% of the heat which was generated as a result of climate change was actually absorbed in the oceans and only under 2% was retained in the atmosphere. It is also estimated that up to 70 meters the oceans had warmed by about $0.11°C$ per decade during the period 1971 to 2010. The effect of warming of the oceans which is now reaching much lower depths would also be a major handicap for human society because in several areas where certain types and stock of fish were available, with climate change, they have and are likely even more to move from one location to the other in order to adapt to the impacts of climate change.

One other major factor which is causing serious problems in the oceans is the problem of acidification. Since the beginning of industrialization and till the period 2010, it is estimated that 30% of the carbon dioxide produced has actually been absorbed by the oceans. As a result of this, there is an increase in acidification of the oceans which represents about a 26% increase. The NRDC (Natural Resources Defence Council) estimates that this extent of acidification has not taken place for over 300 million years. It is also estimated that if we continue on a business as usual path then by the end of the century, the oceans would be 150% more acidic than they are right now. The result of acidification is not only in respect of damage to coral reefs, but also as a result calcium carbonate which is in the oceans, and is the basic ingredient for bones and structural requirements of various marine species would be reduced. This could have very harmful impacts on the growth of marine species over a period of time. It is also obvious that humans would be affected as a result of acidification and warming because there are some species of fish which people living in coastal areas have been catching for their own consumption, and these fish are likely to move away as a result.

The IPCC Special Report on the Ocean and Cryosphere in a Changing Climate warns us appropriately with the following findings:

Since about 1950, many marine species across various groups have undergone shifts in geographical range and seasonal activities in response to ocean warming, sea ice change, and biogeochemical changes, such as oxygen loss, to their habitats. This has resulted in shifts in species composition, abundance, and biomass production of ecosystems from the equator to the poles. Altered interactions between species have caused cascading impacts on ecosystem structure and functioning. In some marine ecosystems, species are impacted by both the effects of fishing and climate changes.

Coastal ecosystems are affected by ocean warming, including intensified marine heatwaves, acidification, loss of oxygen, salinity intrusion and sea level rise, in combination with adverse effects from human activities on ocean and land. Impacts are already observed on habitat area and biodiversity, as well as ecosystem functioning and services.

One major impact of human actions is the extent of pollution with plastics going into every corner of the ocean. It is now well known that if we continue with current levels that by 2050 there would be more plastic than fish in the oceans. It is also now increasingly clear that even thus far almost every form of marine life has ingested plastic in some form or the other, as a result of which there are not only issues of mortality of marine species, but also serious problems, including those related to the health of humans consuming fish that have plastic particles in their bodies.

Another aspect of pollution in the oceans is noise. There is increase in sonar activity through the oceans, including training and other exercises carried out by the navies of the world. This clearly affects marine species, which have been accustomed for millions and thousands of years to a level of silence in the ocean which has direct effects on marine life. Another major factor where increases have taken place in recent years is the extent of offshore activities related to exploration for oil and natural gas resources. With increasing activity in respect of offshore oil production, there has been a substantial increase in drilling activity. This can lead to very serious environmental problems and oil spills, as was the case with the Deep Water Horizon field in the Gulf of Mexico, which led to extensive oil spills being spread not only on the sea but on land as well, where a large number of species actually perished as a result.

Another area that needs to be highlighted as the result of human activities is the extent of sea ice that is available in those areas where there was a substantial quantity of ice before the impacts of climate change resulting from human activities became evident. One major area which is a source of great concern is the extent of ice available in Greenland and the Antarctic ice shelves. It is also now evident that the Arctic region is warming at twice the rate of the rest of the globe, as a result of which Arctic sea ice is vanishing very rapidly, and it is entirely possible that by the middle of the century, in

September of that year, Arctic sea ice would completely vanish, as projected by the IPCC's Fifth Assessment Report. September, as it happens, is a period when, as a result of the heat of the summer, Arctic sea ice melts at much higher levels than during the rest of the year. It would, therefore, be very sad that many of the species available in the Arctic would have vanished in the absence of ice cover on that particular ocean by the year 2050.

Gandhi saw the intermingling of religion, care for the environment, and protection of the earth. He said, "The human species has to realize that Planet Earth with all its life forms can exist without human beings, but human beings cannot exist without Earth and other biota. Earth is our only home."

Enough for Every Man's Needs, but Not Every Man's Greed

Gandhi never believed in preaching what he did not practice but it is for this reason he identified himself in every sense with the suffering masses of India. He stated "Whatever cannot be shared with the masses is taboo to me. My loincloth is an organic evolution in my life. It comes naturally without effort, without premeditation... Service to the poor has been my heart's desire and it has always thrown me amongst the poor and enabled me to identify myself with them... I shall work for an India in which the poorest shall feel that it is their country, in whose making they have an effective voice, an India in which there is no high class or low class of people, an India in which all communities will live in harmony."

There is a story which is now well known and has been repeated by Pete Reilly. He talks about a woman who was very upset that her son was eating too much sugar. Despite exhortations and requests by her he continued to indulge in eating sweets. Finally she decided to go to see his hero, Mahatma Gandhi. When she reached Gandhi, she said, "My son eats too much sugar. It is not good for his health. Would you please advise him to please stop eating it?" Gandhi listened to the woman and spoke to her son, telling him to go home and come back in two weeks. The boy's mother looked perplexed and wondered why he had not asked the boy to stop eating sugar. She took the boy by the hand and went home but came back two weeks later.

Gandhi motioned for them to come forward. He looked directly at the boy, telling him, "Boy, you should stop eating sugar. It is not good for your health." The boy agreed and promised he would not continue with this weakness any longer. The boy's mother turned to Gandhi and asked, "Why didn't you tell him that two weeks ago when I brought him here to see you?" Gandhi smiled and said, "Mother, two weeks ago I was still eating sugar myself." This was the man's integrity and commitment to practicing exactly what he preached.

Gandhi's personal life while it was uniquely sustainable. It was utterly simple, austere, clean, and based entirely on needs. In his own way he derived great comfort from his meagre worldly possessions. In this way, he was able to identify himself with the poorest in the country, and they were, therefore, naturally and irresistibly drawn towards him. Because he preached what he practiced, he always experimented on himself before he shared any experiences with others.

Pope Francis in his sermon on September 1, 2019 highlighted the problem of climate change and the unsustainable nature of human development and lifestyles.

"We have created a climate emergency which seriously threatens nature and life, including our own," he said in a message to mark this year's World Day of Prayer for the Care of Creation.

"This is the time to reflect on our lifestyles and how our daily choices in terms of food, consumption, travel, use of water, energy, and many other material goods are often reckless and harmful."

Mahatma Gandhi, who was the emblem of simplicity and a lifestyle which minimized his own human footprint on the earth, would have been totally in support of the Pope's advice which clearly stated: "Let us choose to change, to take on simpler and more respectful lifestyles!"

The pontiff slammed constant pollution, the incessant use of fossil fuels, intensive agricultural use, and the practice of razing forests to the ground which were raising global temperatures to dangerous levels.

The fundamental question facing human society is whether current trends and practices, apart from being unsustainable, give us the full capacity of happiness that human beings are capable of. One cannot turn back the period of so-called progress but today we have technologies which can clearly reduce our demands on the earth's natural resources and the wealth of nature, which is fundamental to the life not only of human beings but also other species. And our lifestyles must reflect priorities to protect planet Earth. If Gandhi was present today, he would certainly have asked for turning things around, ensuring that instead of pursuing a lust for material things, he would say, in fact, "I need no inspiration other than Nature's. She has never failed me yet. She mystifies me, bewilders me, sends me into ecstasies. Besides God's handiwork, does not man fade into insignificance? Have I not gazed at the marvelous mystery of the starry vault, hardly ever tiring of the great panorama?"

If we had to move rapidly towards the application of Gandhian philosophy and the manner in which it could be applied to current conditions, then clearly, it is important for us to measure the elements of human progress and wellbeing. This is where in recent years there has been considerable effort to define measures by which we could actually measure the progress of human welfare. There is growing disenchantment with the measurement of GDP because this is a measure which has substantial flaws. Some distinguished economists, notably Joseph Stiglitz, have been at the forefront of the effort to redefine progress and move away from the measure of GDP. If we were to look at a major report led by Stiglitz, implemented under the Presidency of Nicolas Sarkozy of France, then we come somewhat close to what Gandhian principles and philosophy define as the welfare of human society.

The Stiglitz report has a number of interesting features that essentially analyze the flaws and the shortcomings of GDP but it also comes up with recommendations that are essentially future oriented. Stiglitz clearly states that statistical indicators are important for designing and assessing policies aiming at advancing the progress of society as well as for assessing and influencing the functioning of economic markets. He also states that more and more people look at statistics to be better informed for making decisions and to respond to the growing demand for information. The supply of statistics has also increased considerably, covering new domains and phenomena. It is well known that what gets measured gets managed and this clearly applies even to an aggregate economic system. Hence, if our measurements are flawed, then decisions will also be distorted, and in the case of any society, if these decisions are flawed or biased, then they could deviate substantially from what constitutes human welfare.

Stiglitz states that choices between promoting GDP and protecting the environment may be false choices once environmental degradation is appropriately included in our measurement of economic performance. Similarly, if we draw inferences about what good policies are by looking at what policies have promoted economic growth, then if our metrics of performance are flawed, those would also affect the inferences that we can draw from such statistics. It is important to come up with the assessment that for much too long, current measures of economic performance have deviated from what might constitute human welfare, since these are based on GDP. Stiglitz mentions that there are even broader concerns about the relevance of these figures as measures of societal wellbeing. He suggests that we are now living in one of the worst financial, economic, and social crises in post-war history. It may be noted that this report was written essentially after the economic crisis of 2008.

The reforms in measurement recommended by the Stiglitz Commission would, therefore, be highly desirable even if we did not have that crisis. Some members of the Commission felt that the crisis only provides an added opportunity to ensure the urgency of these reforms. In particular, the problem of climate change is highlighted in the report, because it is contended that market prices are distorted by the fact that there is no charge imposed on carbon emissions and no account is made of the cost of these emissions in standard national income accounts. It needs to be kept in mind that the risks and the damage that is imposed by the impacts of climate change are directly related to the emissions which have accumulated overtime and the stock of which is responsible for human induced climate change. The report itself is meant to cover various stakeholders in society, whether it is academics and researchers or decision makers in government, business, and industry. It would be useful to get into some of the basic issues which were brought out by the Stiglitz report. One important issue that is highlighted is the fact that the time is ripe for our measurement systems to shift emphasis from measuring economic production to measuring people's wellbeing. And he suggests that measures of wellbeing should be put in the context of sustainability. In this regard, the Stiglitz Commission provides a large number of recommendations, which could be possibly the basis of changes and reforms that have to be brought into the current system of measurement by GDP.

It was in 1930 that Lord Keynes in his essay "The economic possibilities for our grandchildren" stated "For at least another hundred years we must pretend to everyone that fair is foul. Avarice, usury, and precaution must be our Gods for a little longer still. For only they can lead us out of the tunnel of economic necessity and into daylight." He obviously never understood that having released the genie out of the bottle, to put it back was difficult even in ten years, leave alone a hundred.

The first recommendation of the Stiglitz Commission acknowledges the fact that GDP is the most widely used measure of economic activity. There are international standards for its calculation and considerable thought has gone into its statistical and conceptual basis. GDP measures market production, expressed in money units, and as such it is useful. However, according to popular notion, it has been treated as if it were a measure of economic wellbeing, which clearly it is not. Material living standards are more closely associated with measures of net national income, real household income, and consumption. Production can expand while income decreases or vice versa when account is taken of depreciation, income flows into and out of a country, as well as differences between the prices of output and prices of consumer goods. Hence, there is a large range of variables that would provide a sharp deviation between GDP and production and numbers related to production and the very wellbeing of a household or society.

The second recommendation emphasizes the household perspective. The Stiglitz Commission states that citizens' material living standards are better followed through measures of household income and consumption. Indeed, it states that the available national accounts data show that in a number of OECD countries, real household income has grown quite differently from real GDP per capita and typically at a lower rate. The household perspective entails taking account of payments between sectors such as taxes going to government, social benefits coming from government, and interest payments on household loans, which go to financial corporations.

Recommendation 3 suggests that we should consider income and consumption jointly with wealth. A household that spends its wealth on consumption goods increases its current wellbeing, but at the expense of its future wellbeing. The consequences of such behavior would be captured in a household's balance sheet, and the same holds for other sectors of the economy and for the economy as a whole.

Recommendation 4 highlights the provision of much greater prominence to the distribution of income, consumption, and wealth. This is where the Stiglitz Commission comes very close to Gandhian thinking and philosophy. Gandhi believed that distribution of income is a vital means by which the wellbeing of any society can be measured. He also believed that consumption and wealth are an integral part of human welfare taken in the context of income distribution. Another recommendation provided by the Commission is to see that we broaden income measures to include non-market activities. This again is a subject that was very close to Gandhi's heart, mainly because he realized that India at that stage was largely a rural economy and a number of tasks that were performed in the household were essentially not oriented towards market activities. Hence, to minimize the major contribution made by members of a household, women in particular, would clearly be denied the benefits that production in the household actually provides. Stiglitz mentions that while the exclusion from official measures reflects uncertainty about data more than conceptual difficulties, there has been progress in this arena. However, much more needs to be done. We find, for instance, that in some societies household income is taken into account and provided a market value which clearly reduces the disparity between formal income accounting and that which is based on households. If all the unpaid care work done by women across the globe was carried out by a single company, it would have an annual turnover of $ 10 trillion, which is 27 to 43 times that of Apple.

Stiglitz felt that wellbeing is something that cannot be measured on the basis of one single statistic. It is, after all, a function of material living standards that means income, consumption and wealth. It is also a function of health, education, and personal activities, including work, freedom of action, and human rights, which are linked with political voice and governance. Social connections and relationships, the environment (present and future conditions), and insecurity of an economic as well as physical nature clearly define the wellbeing of any society.

One major recommendation is related to the objective and subjective dimensions of wellbeing, which are both extremely important. What is stated is that human welfare and the very value of our lifestyles and living are dependent on objective and subjective dimensions. The recommendation is that steps should be taken to improve measures of people's health, education, personal activities, and environmental conditions. Another important recommendation is that the quality of life indicators in all the dimensions covered should assess inequalities in a comprehensive way. In other words, most dimensions of quality of life require separate measures of inequality but taking into account linkages and correlations, these have to be assessed appropriately. Another recommendation is that surveys should be designed to assess the links between various quality of life domains for each person and this information should be used when designing policies in different fields. It was also suggested that statistical offices should provide the information needed to aggregate across quality of life dimensions. In other words, there has to be a significant amount of empirical research based on all the information that statistical officers possess with them and if these are made available, then this would give us various interpretations of the quality of life. The next recommendation is to see that measures of both objective and subjective wellbeing are made available by those that are responsible for and in possession of statistical information.

An extremely important recommendation is that sustainability assessment requires a well identified dashboard of indicators as the Commission's report suggests. It is recommended that these components of the dashboard should be such that they are interpretable as variations of some underlying stocks. A monetary index of sustainability has its place in such a dashboard but under the current state-of-the-art, it should remain essentially focussed on the economic aspects of sustainability. This recommendation is something that could be questioned because clearly if there is a loss of biodiversity that clearly affects sustainability in its most tangible manner, it cannot be interpreted in terms of economic or monetary value. Hence, perhaps this recommendation needs to be modified and refined such that more value based assessments are carried out. The environmental aspects of sustainability deserve a separate follow up based on a well chosen set of physical indicators. In particular, there is a need for a clear indicator of our proximity to dangerous levels of environmental damage, which has been referred to in the context of climate change or the depletion of fishing stocks. In some sense, this recommendation is at variance with the previous recommendation that emphasizes economic or monetary values.

In a more recent article, Stiglitz referred to the fact that "America has a monopoly problem – and it is huge." There is now widespread concern on the inequitable impacts of capitalism, essentially because the average person on the street is becoming more and more powerless and it is the large corporates and monopoly power which are increasingly dominant in our lives. Stiglitz states "there is much to be concerned about in America today: a growing political and economic divide, slowing growth, decreasing life expectancy, and epidemic of diseases of despair". The author feels that we no longer seem to control our own destinies. He mentions that incidentally, over a century ago, America was, in some ways, at a similar juncture. However, the US passed the Sherman Anti-Trust Act in 1890. However, it appears that in the ensuing decade, anti-trust was taken over by an army of economists and lawyers.

The overall result of this and other trends is that there has been an increase in the market power and concentration of a few firms in various industries, leading to an increase in prices in relation to costs. This, of course, lowers the standard of living very similar to the lowering of wages of workers. Stiglitz feels that the increase in market power can help to expand the slowdown in production growth, the sluggishness of the economy, and the growth of inequality. This is happening despite the fact that the US is today by far the most innovative economy far beyond what existed earlier. The result is that we have today two opposite sets of realization in society, which are perhaps reaching dangerous proportions. There are those who are influenced and are direct beneficiaries of monopoly power and their tentacles reach wide across human society. On the other hand, we have a large number of the masses who feel deprived and powerless to change the government system, even though we realize that the rich are getting richer and the disparity between the privileged and the average citizen is increasing rapidly. The leadership of the political system seems unable to bridge the divide, particularly since most leaders of today rapidly become beholden to those who are the owners of monopoly power. Stiglitz refers to John Kenneth Galbraith and his analysis carried out during the middle of the last century, describing the US economic system as "an economy based on the dominance of large corporations and financial institutions."

In some respect, I think we are approaching a stage where I think what Gandhi had predicted that "a time is coming when those who are in the mad rush today of multiplying their wants, will retrace their steps and say; what have we done … modern civilization is such that one has only to be patient and it will be self-destroyed". To some extent, the voices questioning the current economic system and the unsustainability of all human activities are perhaps the beginning of what Gandhi had predicted. If we look around today, we see hordes of youth who are questioning the inability of leaders and adults in general to deal with the growing challenge of climate change. Clearly the youth who are now very well informed about the scientific assessment of climate change realize fully that their future would suffer essentially because of the growing risks from the impacts of climate change. At the same time, if we were to look at the issue of monopoly power as pointed out by Stiglitz, and which was clearly assessed and warned against by Galbraith during the middle of the last century, gives further weightage to Gandhi's prediction about his view that the West will have to "retrace their steps and say; what have we done?"

It would perhaps be appropriate to look at what Galbraith said in his profoundly important book, "The Affluent Society", which was published in 1958. Recently, The Guardian published an article in which it listed Galbraith's book as one of the hundred best non-fiction books of all time. While referring to "The Affluent Society," this article draws attention to the very first opening line which says "wealth is not without its advantages". It then goes on to mounting an assault on some of the most treasured economic myths of the US. It also highlights the fact that the provocative, humane, and entertaining piece of work that Galbraith had carried out shaped the American mind from the 1950s and 1960s to the fall of the Berlin Wall. However, what has been observed in recent decades is an intensification of the power of corporations and individuals who have concentrated the wealth of every society into their own hands, which certainly goes against the very fundamental view that Gandhi had of the owners of capital interpreting their responsibility as one of trustees on behalf of society as a whole. Galbraith very rightly said "the study of money, above all other fields of economics, is the one in which complexity is used to disguise truth or to evade truth, not to reveal it".

There has apparently been an attempt by those who enjoy the privileges of an affluent society to create some kind of a smoke screen by which they project the fact that human society and its welfare are actually being enhanced even while we see the vicious effects of disparities growing at an alarming rate as mentioned earlier. Galbraith states "as a society becomes increasingly affluent, wants are increasingly created by the process by which they are satisfied". It is interesting to note that today, the expenditure on advertising across the world has reached proportions that would not have been predicted, perhaps even 20 years ago. What is shown below is an increase in advertising expenditure globally in the figure that shows its increase over time, and it requires no great insights to find out that advertising expenditures only increase our wants, as highlighted by Galbraith in his statement.

Figure 2

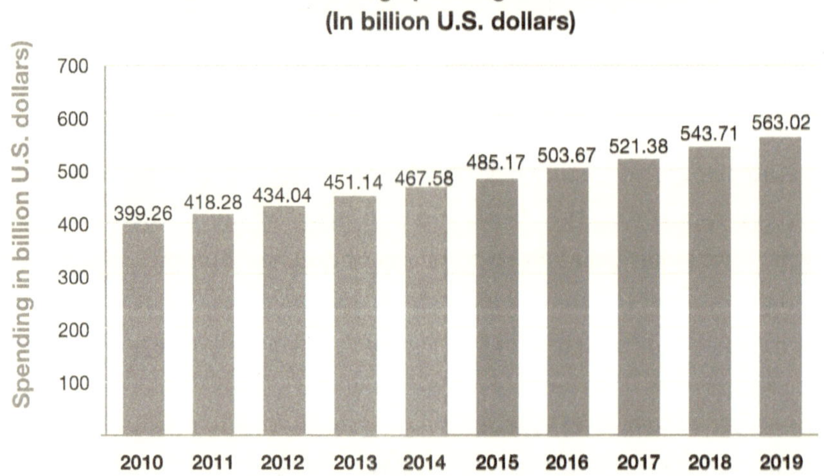

This clearly accords with what Gandhi said about "the mad rush today of multiplying their wants" when referring to the economic system of the West. In an article published in 2017 by the son of John Galbraith, Prof. James Galbraith, who is a distinguished economist in his own right, clearly pointed to the corporate republic that we live in. James Galbraith essentially refers to the fact that we are in some sense moving away from what essentially is the interpretation of economics being based on markets. What he concludes is that the economics of organizations stands in opposition to the economics of markets. This was brought out very clearly by the Senior Galbraith's publication of 1967 which had the title "The New Industrial State". This book came out almost a decade after the enormous success of "The Affluent Society," and by then the Senior Galbraith had observed a trend which, if anything, has intensified in recent years. Galbraith basically stated at the outset that the accepted sequence in economic behavior rarely comes with consumer preferences, which are the first part of the sequence. According to him, firms generally place their products before a discerning public and cater to consumers' sovereignty. They then sell what they can, discount the rest, and then repay to study how it might be done better the next time. The underlying hypothesis behind this is that consumers' sovereignty and preferences by the consumer are the dominant reason why firms produce and provide goods and services in an economic system. However, Galbraith then says that in his view the revised sequence, which he has observed over time, leads to large firms beginning to design and then creating the technology of new production. They then see what is possible and conduct market research on the basis of which they decide what they like. Then, of course, they engage advertising and consumer finance staff to ensure that the result can be obtained. This clearly means that it is the producers of goods and services who are the drivers of activities in an economic system.

The view is also put forward that large business firms often replace the market altogether. They do this by integration: replacing activity previously mediated by open purchase and sale with activity either internal to the corporation or between a large stable enterprise and its small specialized suppliers to whom risk is transferred. This interpretation accords with the whole problem with GDP which, as Stiglitz has rightly mentioned, is driven by production since it does not necessarily go into other aspects of economic wellbeing. Since GDP has, in a sense, become a sort of religion with decision makers and those who study and report on economic activity, it is the suppliers of goods and services who are treated with a high level of respect by those who regard GDP as the ultimate in assessing economic activity. It is interesting to refer to what Lord Keynes stated in 1930 in his essay entitled "Economic Possibilities for our Grandchildren" as quoted earlier, part of which extolled what Gandhi regarded as contemptible, namely, "Avarice, usury, and precaution must be our gods for a little longer still". Perhaps even Lords Keynes did not realize the intensity with which the gods that he is referring to would multiply our wants and create disparities as well as a system which relies entirely on production that deviates from human welfare in its normal sense. It is to be seen whether, by 1930, Lord Keynes and his advocacy to let God continue for a little longer, perhaps for at least another 100 years, as he mentioned, will actually lead to a collapse and a reduction of reliance on GDP. The rate at which concerns and a deep desire to alter the current system is moving ahead, it may be possible that by the time we reach 2030, we would have a very different set of economic indicators which supplant and replace GDP as the ultimate god.

Gandhi himself had a deep fascination for everything related to nature. He has been quoted as saying, "I need no inspiration other than Nature's. She has never failed me yet. She mystifies me, bewilders me, sends me into ecstasies. Besides God's handiwork, does not man fade into insignificance? When I admire the wonders of a sunset or the beauty of the moon, my soul expands in the worship of the creator".

He also in a very profound, though subtle way, warned against the plunder or destruction of natural assets on which he stated, "We may utilize the gifts of Nature just as we choose but in Her books, the debits are always equal to the credits."

One hopes that by 2030, if not earlier, we might have a set of indicators that essentially embody the very basic desire of human beings to be able to achieve happiness and to be able to enjoy the very essentials of what constitutes spiritual and mental fulfillment. In essence, therefore, it would be very important for us to focus on and identify the desire for human relationships, whether it is friends, family, or society at large, as well as to be able to get access to the gifts of nature which unfortunately, with the growth of urbanized existence, has been completely overshadowed by our desire for products and goods that are part of the system which measures GDP.

****

Human capital and inequality
by
Dr. Rashmi Pachauri Rajan

Gandhiji said, "A technological society has two choices. First, it can wait until catastrophic failures expose systemic deficiencies, distortion, and self-deception. Second, a culture can provide social checks and balances to correct for systemic distortion prior to catastrophic failures."

Ananya, the daughter, the Lakshmi of the household! She was bright, beautiful, and intelligent. She scored the highest marks in her class, an ace student, one who everyone thought was going to be the crowning glory of her school, who was going to have her name up in bold letters wherever she went and whatever she did! And it was her father who taught her to be the best, to do the best, to know that life was either a success or a failure – 100 percent was success and 99 percent was failure! And that was her *mantra*. She wanted to become a doctor. It had been her passion ever since she could remember. She couldn't wait to pass school and join medical college and then go on to specialize in cardiology. The only hitch was that her father had made it very clear to her that she was only going to be allowed to do that if her scores were high enough in her Board Exams to make her eligible to sit for her medical entrance exams. Otherwise, she would follow the age-old tradition of joining an Arts College, graduate, and then be married off. Oh, of course, she could pursue a "career" as a teacher or something along those lines… if her future in-laws and husband permitted it!

Ananya was one of two children, her older brother being the other. Dhruv was the apple of his father's eye, the one who could do no wrong – even if his marks were nowhere near his sister's, even if he was frequently in trouble because of his behavior in school or within the neighborhood ("he's a child, and after all, boys will be boys!") – because he was the son of the family, the one who would take the *'kul'* forward! His future was assured. He would take over the family business, a thriving jewellery business, famous in their town, and even to an extent in the country. This was fine with Dhruv as he, in any case, had no great career ambitions, and this would allow him to follow his vagaries since the business was, by now, more or less, running on its own.

And so, the exams came, and Ananya diligently burned the midnight oil, studied, and plodded through them. On the whole, she felt she had done well – a bit of a glitch in one of the papers, but nothing to get over-concerned about. A month later the results were announced. Ananya stood before the notice board adjacent to the Principal's office, along with noisy crowd of her classmates. She scanned the names on the top of the list, assured that hers would be the first. Adhaar, Manav, Seema… where was her name? Oh, here it was… Ananya… 95 percent! Ninety-five percent… not a 100 percent, not even 99 percent… 95 percent! She turned and fled. Running all the way home, she knew for certain that she could never make it into any of the acknowledged medical colleges! Not with a mere 95 percent, not when she knew that even people with 98 percent found it difficult to do so! It was over for her!

"Become a doctor. You will earn loads of money. You will be respected and worshipped... a god in a white coat... you will have it made!"

"You can start a private practice... make sure you have the cream of the city's crowd as your patients."

"And then we will find a boy worthy of you... from a rich family who would never have the courage to ask for the dowry they would otherwise demand!"

"You will be their prized possession! The bahu who is one in a million!"

She had listened to this twaddle, knowing deep in her heart that she just had to listen, grin and bear it for the time being. Because she had always known what she really wanted – to become a renowned, well-respected, honorable cardiologist who would save lives, do research and make break-throughs, and who would follow her heart, regardless of what other people's motivations for her were.

But now it was over, truly over! She had not made the 100 percent mark that was so very important in the life of students today. So very important that a child study by rote, know every word on every page, please the teacher who is the would-be maker or breaker of her life. So very important that the student know the "method" of answering exam papers… not necessarily the subject or content… but know "how to" answer the questions. And somewhere in that oh, so important process, Ananya had failed – with a 95 percent she had failed! And so, she had failed in life!

She had not obtained the required marks that would assure her entrance into a good medical school. And even though Ananya had the passion, dedication, and perseverance, and would have, over time acquired the needed skills, within this prevalent education system, there were others who lacked all of this but would secure the limited seats available and then go on to become doctors, good, bad, or indifferent.

What she did not realize is that it was not SHE who had failed, it was the system who had failed HER! The system that was supposed to have focussed on her overall development, on the development of her as a person, a good human being endowed with "self-reverence, self-knowledge, and self-control, with emphasis on duty, welfare and moral, social, psychological and political knowledge." This system had miserably failed her. She had not read Mahatma Gandhi's views on education. She did not know that he firmly believed that, "The real difficulty is that people have no idea of what education truly is. We assess the value of education in the same manner as we assess the value of land or of shares in the stock exchange market. We want to provide only such education as would enable the student to earn more. We hardly give any thought to the improvement of the character of the educated. The girls, we say, do not have to earn, so why should they be educated? As long as such ideas persist, there is no hope of our ever knowing the true value of education." (M. K. Gandhi True Education on the National Council for Teacher Education site).

And all the 'advice' she had been getting all her life with respect to the 'value' of her medical degree was based on this education system, which was geared to making money, not gaining an education. All of this happened in this universe, with today's education system in which: marks = literacy (not necessarily education) = money/success.

But let us move to a parallel universe. Let us transport ourselves to a universe which adopted Gandiji's philosophy of education. Gandhi favored an education system with far greater emphasis on learning skills in practical and useful work, one that included physical, mental, and spiritual studies. The fundamental aspect of Gandhiji's proposal on education was the introduction of productive handicrafts in the school curriculum. He believed that knowledge of the production processes involved in crafts, such as spinning, weaving, leather-work, pottery, metal-work, basket-making, and bookbinding, had always been the monopoly of specific caste groups in the lowest stratum of the traditional social hierarchy. Many of those belonging to these castes fell into the category of 'untouchables.' The colonial education system introduced later emphasized skills such as literacy and acquisition of knowledge over which the upper castes had a monopoly. Gandhi's basic views on education, therefore, embodied his perception of an ideal society consisting of small, self-reliant communities, with his ideal citizen being an industrious, self-respecting, and generous individual living in a small cooperative community. Gandhi called his ideas *'Nai Talim'* (which literally translates into 'new education'). He believed that the Western style of education debased and destroyed Indigenous cultures. A different basic education model, he believed, would lead to better self-awareness, encourage people to treat all work as equally respectable and valued, and lead to a society with less social diseases. He said, "By education, I mean an all-round drawing out of the best in child and man – body, mind, and spirit. Literacy is not the end of education, not even the beginning. It is one of the means whereby men and women can be educated. Literacy in itself is no education." He propounded an education system that aimed at educating the whole person and not just certain aspects of the person. For Gandhi, education was, in and of itself, a highly moral activity. This reflected the ultimate goal of education in the ancient Indian education system - which was the overall development of students.

Gandhi explained the aim of education as not only developing good individuals but also individuals who understand their responsibilities. This, again, is closely related to the Hindu concept of *varnashrama dharma* (a person's responsibility regarding class (*varna*) and stage of life (*ashrama*). When one understands his or her responsibilities, it will lead to the spirit of social consciousness and social mindedness (https://www.mkgandhi.org/articles/g_edu.htm).

Gandhiji's philosophy on education was strongly reflected in the Kothari Commission's recommendation (1964-66) for work experience in school education as an integral part of the curriculum. The report observed that "In our country, a revolutionary experiment was launched by Mahatma Gandhi in the form of basic education. The concept of work-experience is essentially similar. It described his educational thinking in terms of a society launched on the road to industrialization." (https://archive.org/stream/ReportOfTheEducationCommission1964-66D.S.KothariReport/48.Jp-ReportOfTheEducationCommission1964-66d.s.kothari_djvu.txt)

So, in essence, for Mohandas Karamchand Gandhi, knowledge of and oneness with God, self-realization and spiritualism was the ultimate aim of education. This, he felt would liberate the body, mind, and soul, which meant liberation from economic, social, and political slavery. He said, "True education should result, not in the material power, but in spiritual-force".

So, in this parallel universe, even with a 95 percent, the education system and its natural process would give Ananya the opportunity to take an entrance exam for a medical career. It would enable her to express her passion and aptitude for this career path and to show her desire for learning, and thus, assure her admission into a good medical school. She would develop into a successful cardiologist, success being measured in this universe by her dedication, sincerity, and honor towards working to enhance and save lives, to give back and contribute to society, and to spiritually augment herself into a higher soul and, thus, attain liberation and *Nirvana.* In this world, Ananya would use her passion and her skills to integrate the advantages that today's fast-developing technology has to offer (which is nigh impossible to ignore or avoid), with the tenets of Gandhiji's educational philosophy to help the poorest and weakest in the society in improving their health and overall wellbeing, which would, in the longer term, boost and encourage the development of grass-root communities to bring about self-sufficiency and autonomy more widely.

Ananya, in this universe, would be a success! She would be "the change she wanted to see in this world."

No Inspiration Other Than Nature's

Paul Bloom, a very distinguished psychologist at Yale University who has explored and studied the very basics of human happiness, is absolutely right when he says, "There is something primal about our need for nature – for time in the outdoors, for sunshine, for fresh air". Paul Bloom writes that our hunger for the natural world is everywhere and that people like to be close to oceans, mountains, and trees. He states that in the most urban environment, this primal need is reflected in real estate prices. For instance, if you want a view of the trees of Central Park in New York, it will cost you. Similarly, office buildings in urban areas set up atriums and keep plants indoors. We also give flowers to the sick and the beloved and return home to watch Animal Planet and the Discovery Channel. He feels that many of us seek to escape our manufactured environment whenever we can. That is why we enjoy hiking, camping, traveling by canoe, or, for that matter, even hunting.

Paul Bloom mentions that on the heels of the study that came out saying that teenagers spend up to 7.5 hours per day on digital devices, which is an hour above the previous year, he wondered whether what is happening to our individual relationships to the natural world is a result of technology. He feels that we care about nature essentially for our own sake because it happens to make us happy or healthy. He feels that few people would need convincing that the destruction of rainforests, the mass extinction of species, and the melting of the ice sheet in Greenland would all be very bad things. He then asks whether we should list the reasons and he feels that we should. He laments the fact that our species has already kissed nature goodbye and some feel that we are better off for it. Technology as a result has come to be more diverse than the biosphere. He refers to Karl Marx who observed in 1867 that there were 500 types of hammers made in Birmingham, England. In 1988, Donald Norman, a cognitive scientist at the University of California in San Diego, suggested that the average American encounters 20000 different kinds of artifacts in everyday life. This, of course, is substantially more than the number of animals and plants that we can distinguish and right now there are about 1.5 million identified species on earth. This, of course, may seem impressive but it is nothing compared to the more than 7 million United States patents.

Paul Bloom feels that our hunger for the natural is everywhere. It is reflected in art, but the appeal of nature is also reflected in where we most want to live. He feels that people like to live close to oceans mountains, and trees and even in the most urban environment you find people have a preference for real estate that is close to some form of nature. Overall, therefore, the preservation of the natural world should be important to us. The question is how important. Paul Bloom refers to the psychologist Philip Tetlock and points out that many people talk about the environment as a sacred value, protected from utilitarian trade-offs. When the Exxon Valdez spilled nearly 11 million gallons of crude oil, 80% of the respondents in one poll supposedly said that we should pursue greater environmental protection regardless of cost.

If we refer to some age-old practices, for instance, such as sacred groves, which were prevalent and still are to some extent in parts of India, the people give up a great deal to forego the benefits of forests and minor forests produce, just because they regard certain groves as sacred. These are not to be touched and, therefore, clearly involve an opportunity cost which the community is willing to bear and they thus prefer to gain the pleasures and the benefits of untouched forests confined to these sacred groves. The fact that urban existence, which is growing rapidly, clearly limits our access to nature, even if we may be close to Central Park or might have an atrium located in the urban offices where we work. Hence, it would perhaps make a great deal of sense to think in terms of moving away from an urbanized existence and perhaps think in terms of going back to rural locations. This would also allow us to tend to natural beauty around us and perhaps plant trees and to nurture them as they grow, thus make sure that they improve and refine human existence in a manner that has existed for the entire period that human beings have inhabited this earth.

The Greater Good magazine has published an article with the title "How nature can make you kinder, happier, and more creative," authored by Jill Suttie. The author believes that hiking in nature has many psychological benefits, even though she did not have much science to back up this belief. However, scientists it appears are now beginning to find evidence that being in nature has a profound impact on people's brains and behavior, helping them to reduce anxiety, brooding, and stress, and increase their attention capacity, creativity, and ability to connect with other people. A researcher in the University of Utah has also mentioned that research is now beginning to see changes in the brain and changes in the body that suggest that we are physically and mentally more healthy when we are interacting with nature. Unfortunately, however, most people these days, and certainly those living in urban locations, are spending more and more time indoors and online, which is particularly the case with children. And if the claims of scientists are valid there is need to preserve natural space, including those in urban locations, and of course in the wild. When Gandhi was asked what he thought about wild life, his response was "wild life is decreasing in the jungles, but it is increasing in the towns".

There are various benefits of being in nature, which the author of the Greater Good Magazine article puts forward.

The first relates to the finding that being in nature decreases stress. It quotes a recent research experiment conducted in Japan measuring the heart rate variability, heart rate, and blood pressure of all participants who were assigned to walk in a forest as opposed to an urban center. The participants were also asked to fill out a questionnaire about their moods, stress levels, and other psychological indicators. The result clearly showed that those who walked in the forest had a beneficial effect on stress reduction, far beyond what exercise alone would have produced. Other studies also carried out in Finland and at the Texas A&M University and many others, provide overwhelming evidence that being in natural spaces, or even just looking out of a window on to a natural scene, somehow soothes us and relieves stress.

Another great benefit of being close to nature is that it makes you happier and less brooding. In a study carried out at Stanford University in 2015, the results showed that those who walked in nature experienced less anxiety, rumination, and negative effects, as well as more positive emotions in comparison to urban walkers. They were also able to improve their performance on memory tasks. In another study, the same researchers were able to zero in on how walking in nature affects rumination, which has been associated with the onset of depression and anxiety. Participants who took a 90-minute walk in either a natural setting or an urban location had their brains scanned before and after their walks and were surveyed on self-reported rumination levels. The essential result was that participants who walked in a natural setting versus those in an urban setting reported decreased rumination after the walk and showed increased activity in that part of the brain whose deactivation is associated with depression and anxiety. The researcher at Stanford University believes that "Ecosystem services are being incorporated into decision-making at all levels of public policy, land use planning, urban design, and it's very important to be sure to incorporate empirical findings from psychology into their decisions."

The third benefit of being close to nature is that it relieves attention fatigue and increases creativity. The researcher, quoted by the author, mentions that "When you use your cell phone to talk, text, shoot photos, or whatever else you can do with your cell phone, you're tapping the prefrontal cortex and causing reductions in cognitive resources." In a 2012 study, this team of researchers showed that hikers on a four-day backpacking trip could solve significantly more puzzles requiring creativity when compared to a control group of people waiting to take the same hike, and, in fact, the difference was 47 % more.

Another important finding is that nature may help you to be kind and generous. In a series of experiments published in 2014, a group of researchers at the University of California, Berkeley, studied the potential impact of nature on the willingness to be generous, trusting, and helpful toward others, while considering what factors might influence that relationship. The participants in this experiment were exposed to more or less subjectively beautiful nature scenes and were then observed how participants behaved playing two economics games. Those exposed to the more beautiful nature scenes acted more generously and were more trusting in the games than those who saw less beautiful scenes. Several other experiments and studies confirm this conclusion.

Another finding is that nature makes you feel more alive. The researcher quoted over here suggested that there is something about nature that keeps us psychologically healthy, since nature is a resource which is generally free and one that can be accessed at least in those locations which are close to it. Thus, even in urban areas, we need to provide parks and green spaces.

Gandhi emphasized the development of villages clearly so that the benefit of being close to nature and the sustainable use of natural resources can be achieved as opposed to those living in urban spaces who are increasingly becoming victims of slum living and residents of shanty towns.

Gandhi stated "Of all the animal creations of God, man is the only animal who has been created in order that he may know his Maker. Man's aim in life is not, therefore, to add from day-to-day to his material prospects and to his material possessions, but his predominant calling is from day-to-day to come nearer his own Maker." Nature clearly reminds every human being of the gift of creation which, of course, is so much superior to the assets of urban infrastructure and facilities no matter how these have been constructed or how brilliant the architecture involved is.

It is interesting to see the distinction between countries and their forested areas. Those with the highest area under forest are generally the countries of Europe. South America, which is home to the Amazon rainforest, has 21% of the planet's forest cover. North and Central America are 3rd with around 18% of forests which are spread generally over Canada and the U.S. Ten of the most forest rich countries account for 2/3rd of the world's forest cover with 34% of the remainder being distributed among all the remaining countries. The Russian Federation alone has 20% of the world's forest cover but ranks 53rd among the most forested countries because of its large size of total landmass under its control. Generally, between 2000 and 2010, deforestation has decreased global forest cover by a huge quantity of 13 million hectares. Yet, because of human encroachment on forested land, particularly for purposes of expanding agricultural land, we remain totally indifferent to decreasing forest cover. Gandhi rightly said, "To me, art, in order to be truly great, must, like the beauty of Nature, be universal in its appeal. It must be simple in its presentation and direct in its expression, like the language of nature. When I admire the wonders of a sunset or the beauty of the moon, my soul expands in the worship of the creator." Many years before Gandhi, Chief Seattle extolled the beauty of nature and lamented the fact that "There is no quiet place in the white man's cities. No place to hear the unfurling of leaves in spring or the rustle of an insect's wings. And what is there to life if a man cannot hear the lonely cry of a whippoorwill or the argument of the frogs around a pond at night."

In our desire and craving for material goods, which modern society has concentrated on driven by advertisements and a mindless obsession of "keeping up with the Joneses", we are overwhelmed with excessive supplies. Hence, in urban areas, human society is clearly losing the benefits of being close to nature.

In our current predicament of excessive and wasteful consumption, we need to redefine growth by moving from urban to rural locations. However, this will not happen if public policy only favors investments in infrastructure and facilities for urban locations while at the same time depriving rural areas of a fair share that they are entitled to receive, which cumulative deficiencies over the years have now made imperative.

Capital as Such is Not Evil, it is its Wrong Use

What Lord Keynes regarded as a measure of human progress, namely the growth of GDP, extending well into a century and more as a growing obsession for human society could easily end very soon. The gathering voices, which have begun questioning the excessive reliance on GDP across the world, could suddenly result in a cataclysmic shift with a massive power to disrupt the growing trends of the past. After all, Gandhi did say "A small body of determined spirits fired by an unquenchable faith in their mission can alter the course of history". We have seen the flaws associated with computation of GDP, but more significant perhaps is human society's obsession with the growth in this indicator as the be-all and end-all of human efforts.

While there are substantial merits in a more idyllic form of existence that seem beyond our reach today, that perhaps is not the only rationale for ensuring that we move towards the implementation and acceptance of Gandhian philosophy worldwide. A more urgent, and perhaps in some sense a more dire reason for moving quickly, almost on a tectonic basis, towards Gandhi's philosophical thinking is to ensure that the risks which are confronting us today do not overwhelm us and do not in any way endanger the existence of human society and other species which are living on this planet.

It would be interesting to refer to an interesting piece of work by Jason Hickel of the University of London, published as issue no. 87 in the Real-World Economics Review. Hickel appropriately starts by referring to what he calls a climate crisis and how it worsens with carbon budgets set out by the Paris Agreement actually shrinking. He believes that climate scientists and ecologists have increasingly come to highlight economic growth as a matter of concern. According to him, growth drives the energy demand up and makes it significantly more difficult to deal with the climate crisis. It needs to be noted, however, that economic growth is not necessarily inextricably linked with a proportionate growth in energy demand. We have several examples of countries, more or less at the same level of affluence and somewhat similar geographical spread and climatic conditions, actually producing much more by way of GDP and economic output with the same quantum of energy as would be the case with some other countries. In other words, there are huge disparities at every level of the scale of economic development between countries and communities in the efficiency of energy use.

Nevertheless, it is important to revert to Hickel's major thesis which he refers to as degrowth. In recent times, a number of economists, particularly those who are now growing in number as ecological economists, highlight the need for implementing degrowth worldwide, which most persons would regard as an approach which essentially reduces aggregate economic activity as currently measured by GDP. As would be shown later in this volume, there is absolutely no reason why we should settle on degrowth or a reduction in aggregate economic activity as the approach by which we bring about a reduction in the emissions of carbon dioxide. In actual fact, growth, which is based on today's pattern of development, needs to be replaced with something far more sustainable and far more friendly to human society and other species and the planet at large, which we would illustrate through several sets of actions and approaches that would be required.

Hickel then refers to the Paris Agreement on climate change and the fact that the Intergovernmental Panel on Climate Change (IPCC) has brought out a special report which assesses the scientific basis for increase in average temperature by 2100 being limited to 1.5°C over preindustrial levels. This particular report specifies that in order to limit temperature increase to 1.5°C, we would have to reduce global emissions to half their value by 2030 and these would then need to reach net zero level by the middle of the century. In actual fact, the higher level of assurance that this special report provides relates to decarbonizing the economic system by 2040 preferably a decade before 2050. Hence, there is clearly a need to reduce the emissions of carbon dioxide perhaps far more rapidly than the somewhat lower probability approach of reaching this level by 2050 would imply. It is entirely true that as far back as the Fourth Assessment Report of the IPCC, it was actually assessed that even to reach the 2-degree limit by the end of the century, GHG emissions would have to peak by 2020 at the latest. We are at the doorstep of 2020, and if one was to go by measurements of GHG emissions in 2018, we have certainly not reached the level where 2020 might actually yield a peak in emissions, beyond which possibly we would have to be able to reduce them quite rapidly.

There is also a need to look at carbon capture and storage. In fact, in the Fifth Assessment Report of the IPCC, it was brought out very clearly that one measure that would perhaps be desirable is the use of BECCS, which means bioenergy with carbon capture and storage. However, leaving aside these technical discussions, what is far more important is to see how we might be able to focus on the issue of degrowth as the term that it is understood to represent. The most important objective of degrowth is basically to bring down the throughput of materials and energy right across the global economy and ensure that high income nations with high levels of per capita consumption bring this about far more rapidly and, therefore, in quantitative terms far more effectively than the developing countries. The latter would, of course, have to ensure that they are able to do this in an innovative manner as they tread a path which does not necessarily emulate the path of the developed world but ensures that far greater technological innovations and all round reduction of high intensity energy use is avoided. This would enable the developing countries to move along the path of development which is far more sustainable. All of this also requires that we bring about a deliberate and more equitable distribution of existing income. According to Hickel, by distributing existing income more fairly, we can improve human welfare and accomplish social objectives without growth. This, of course, may certainly raise the issue of those who regard degrowth and reduction in emissions of carbon dioxide and other GHGs as a manifestation of Marxist philosophy. However, the issue in question right now is not that redistributing income is in itself being attempted to achieve some Marxist or socialist objective. The issue at hand is really that which requires a reduction in GHG emissions, which would be achieved far better if there is a redistribution of income.

Perhaps the most important component of Hickel's analysis goes into the history of what one might describe as the capitalist form of economic growth. Hickel, of course, starts by saying that it could be argued that economic growth is necessary for mobilizing resources to invest in the technological change required to shift the world towards sustainability. This, no doubt, is true given the fact that we have a large area of technological developments and an economic system based on technologies that are essentially highly energy intensive. And, in many such cases, energy use is based on the use of fossil fuels and these are far more carbon intensive in nature than viable options available today. It, of course, is also true as Gandhi rightly mentioned, we must also modify our demand for goods, which are part of our consumption patterns today, because beyond a point, in Gandhi's view, these do not in any way add to human welfare and perhaps are the most important means by which we can reduce the demand for goods and consequently the demand for fuels that generate carbon dioxide.

Hickel then takes us through the history of the capitalist system. He says that, for instance, in a city like London, house prices are astronomically high. These prices, he believes, are fictional and they have no indication of the actual cost of building a house or even of the land on which it is built, but are rather largely a consequence of the rapid privatization of the public housing stock in Britain since 1980, as well as those related to financial regulations, the zero interest rate policy, and other factors. He thinks that there is a problem which is as old as capitalism itself. He goes back to what is known as the Statute of Merton of 1235 – which fenced off the commons and systematically forced peasants off the land in a violent, centuries long campaign of dispossession. What this specifies in very sharp terms is essentially what Gandhi was truly conscious of with violence by one group of society on another who possibly did not have the means, the weapons, or the ability to fight those who were in power.

Hickel states that this period saw the abolition of the ancient right to habitation once enshrined in the Charter of the Forest, which guaranteed ordinary people access to land, forests, game, fodder, waters, fish, and other resources necessary for existence. It is interesting to see that the situation which Hickel describes is, in some sense, similar to how communities and forest dwellers in India were dispossessed by the colonial power simply because the latter put forward the view that communities were incapable of ensuring the sustainable maintenance and growth of forest resources in the country. This, as mentioned earlier, was only a ruse by which the colonial power was able to gain direct access and rights over forest resources which were acquired essentially for a range of economic activities in Great Britain.

However, going back to the period of the Right to Habitation being abolished, Hickel states that England's commoners found themselves subject to a new regime and in order to survive, they had to compete with each other for leases to farm on newly privatized land. He states that leases were allocated on the basis of productivity, and were reassessed at regular intervals. In order to retain these leases, peasants had to find ways to intensity their production vis-à-vis their competitors. In other words, this was really not very different from deployment of slave labor because with the intense competition that was set in as a result of the revised conditions, there was clearly a compulsion on the part of labor to produce more and more, otherwise they would lose access to land and face starvation.

Hickel states that this whole process was essentially to create a capitalist surplus of profit. Capitalism, according to him, always needs an outside source external to itself, from which it can draw uncompensated value. But, according to him, there is also something else at stake, something even more important, more powerful, and perhaps as a more dynamic force. He felt that the emergence of the enormous productive capacity that characterizes capitalism depended in the first instance on subjecting humans to artificial scarcity. In other words, by driving out those who had the right to habitation, the more prosperous and the more powerful created a sense of scarcity and the threat of hunger which produced intense competition. And, this, of course, was done alongside the process of elite accumulation. It is also relevant to recall that this was enforced by state violence, which included peasant uprisings against enclosures and these were repeatedly put down by force and often by massacre.

Here again, we need to understand Gandhi's interpretation of what consti-tutes current day capitalism because in its roots lies the initial exploitation by one small group of prosperous individuals of a much larger group of underprivileged commoners who had no choice but to seek leases from the scarce land which was artificially created by those in power. Feudalism in various parts of the world had similar characteristics. Hickel also says that in India, British colonizers sought to find ways to compel Indians to shift from subsistence farming to cash crops for export. Interestingly, in the large state of Bihar, which till the time of colonization was one of the most prosperous regions in the country, farmers were persuaded to move to indigo plantation, the product of which was shipped to Great Britain since white clothes at that point had to have a tinge of indigo that came essentially from India. This was also assisted to a great extent by maintaining a feudal order in the state of Bihar where the privileged played into the hands of the colonial rulers and ensured that the peasants were dispossessed much like was the case historically in Britain. In Hickel's view, capitalism transforms even the most spectacular productivity gains, not into abundance and human freedom, but into new forms of artificial scarcity. He, therefore, feels that there would be risks to shutting down the engine of accumulation itself, and therefore, killing of the goose that lays the golden egg if we were to forego the artificial scarcity which is created by the current capitalist system.

It is interesting that Hickel refers to the 1970s when the United States had a lower poverty rate, higher average real wages, and higher happiness levels than it has today, despite having less than half of today's per capita income. The difference has to do with distribution. He contends that in the 1970s, income was shared more fairly, leading to better social outcomes. Virtually all the benefits of growth since 1980 have been accumulated by the rich leaving the rest of society in a state of what can be called artificial scarcity.

All of this may tend some people to believe that perhaps we have to get away from capitalism and the only forms of government that we know of in recent times is the practice of communism or an extreme form of socialism. This, of course, would be a case of throwing the baby out with the bath water because we know the evils of communism. We have seen how it subjugates the human spirit and how a centralized authority, which is an essential part of introducing and implementing communist dogma, can actually commit crimes against human beings. Large scale spread of misery has characterized, for instance, the period that the Soviet Union was under communist rule and, of course, there are several other examples that could also be quoted. Gandhi was as such not against the use of capital, and therefore, he was thinking of a humane means by which capital could be employed in a manner that does not exploit one class versus the other, and in a manner that ensures some form of distributive justice as far as income and wealth are concerned and by which we would ensure that the last man, that means his concept of *Antyodaya* which reflected on our actions providing benefits to the most underprivileged and the most dispossessed human beings who are part of society.

In this context, he said, "recall the face of the poorest and the weakest man you may have seen and ask yourself if the step you contemplate to take is going to be of any use to him. Will he gain anything by it?" If capitalists ignore the objectives of equity, then it is not following this principle of *Antyodaya*. Gandhi, in fact, quoted, "capital as such is not evil; it is its wrong use that is evil". Hence, what Gandhi was looking for was the deployment of capital in a manner that does not necessarily create the evil of the rich getting richer and the poor remaining exactly where they were or perhaps even becoming worse off as a result of the contrived scarcity that they were subjected to. Gandhi also highlighted the need for capital when he said "capital in some form or the other will always be needed". This means that he was fully aware of how capital can actually create a just, humane, and an egalitarian society where the needs and wants of the most dispossessed could be looked after through the deployment and use of capital to improve their wellbeing.

Gandhi equated the true practice of democracy as a non-violent system of government and stated that "the wide gulf between the rich and the hungry millions would make it impossible to achieve such a non-violent system of government. He said, "The contrast between the palaces of New Delhi and the miserable hovels of the poor, laboring class cannot last one day in a free India in which the poor will enjoy the same power as the richest in the land. A violent and bloody revolution is a certainty one day unless there is a voluntary abdication of riches and the power that riches give and sharing them for the common good. I adhere to my doctrine of trusteeship in spite of the ridicule that has been poured upon it." He believed fervently in power being provided to the people at the bottom most levels of the government. He stated that "The greater the power of the *panchayats*, the better for the people." He further stated, "If we would see our dream of *Panchayat Raj*, i.e., true democracy realized, we would regard the humblest and lowest Indian as being equally the ruler of India with the tallest in the land…. This presupposes that all are pure or will become pure if they are not. …..And purity must go hand-in-hand with wisdom."

Unfortunately, the form of government that Gandhi had in mind has gradually withered away even where it existed. We find increasingly that the power of the vested interests and corporate entities is driving policies formulated by governments and which go against the interest of the people, humanity at large, and the sustainability of nature as well as this planet.

Nowhere is this clearer than in the case of the fossil fuel industry, which benefits from enormous subsidies, despite the fact that carbon dioxide emissions from fossil fuels are resulting in climate change which is becoming increasingly dangerous. The International Monetary Fund (IMF) brought out a study on May 2, 2019 entitled "Global Fossil Fuel Subsidies Remain Large: An Update Based on Country-Level Estimates". This study estimates global subsidies at a staggering level, even though the global community is fully aware of the imperative need to cut down on CO2 emissions. An extract from the summary of the study is provided below:

"Globally, subsidies remained large at $4.7 trillion (6.3 percent of global GDP) in 2015 and are projected at $5.2 trillion (6.5 percent of GDP) in 2017. The largest subsidizers in 2015 were China ($1.4 trillion), United States ($649 billion), Russia

($551 billion), European Union ($289 billion), and India ($209 billion). About three quarters of global subsidies are due to domestic factors—energy pricing reform thus remains largely in countries' own national interest—while coal and petroleum together account for 85 percent of global subsidies. Efficient fossil fuel pricing in 2015 would have lowered global carbon emissions by 28 %and fossil fuel air pollution deaths by 46 %, and increased government revenue by 3.8 % of GDP."

The scientific community has been warning us for well over a century on the dangers of continuing with emissions of CO2. As early as the 1890s, a Swedish scientist, Arrhenius, solved hundreds of equations and came up with clear projections on how continued emissions of CO2 would lead to climate change. In November 1965, it has been reported by an article in the Guardian that US President Lyndon Johnson released a report authored by the "Environmental Pollution Panel of the President's Science Advisory Committee," which brought out the likely impact of continued fossil fuel production on global warming. It is generally believed that the oil companies were aware of the scientific reality of climate change as early as the 1950s but despite their understanding of climate change and the link with CO2 emissions, they had continued with maximizing production and increasing their profits.

Figure 3.

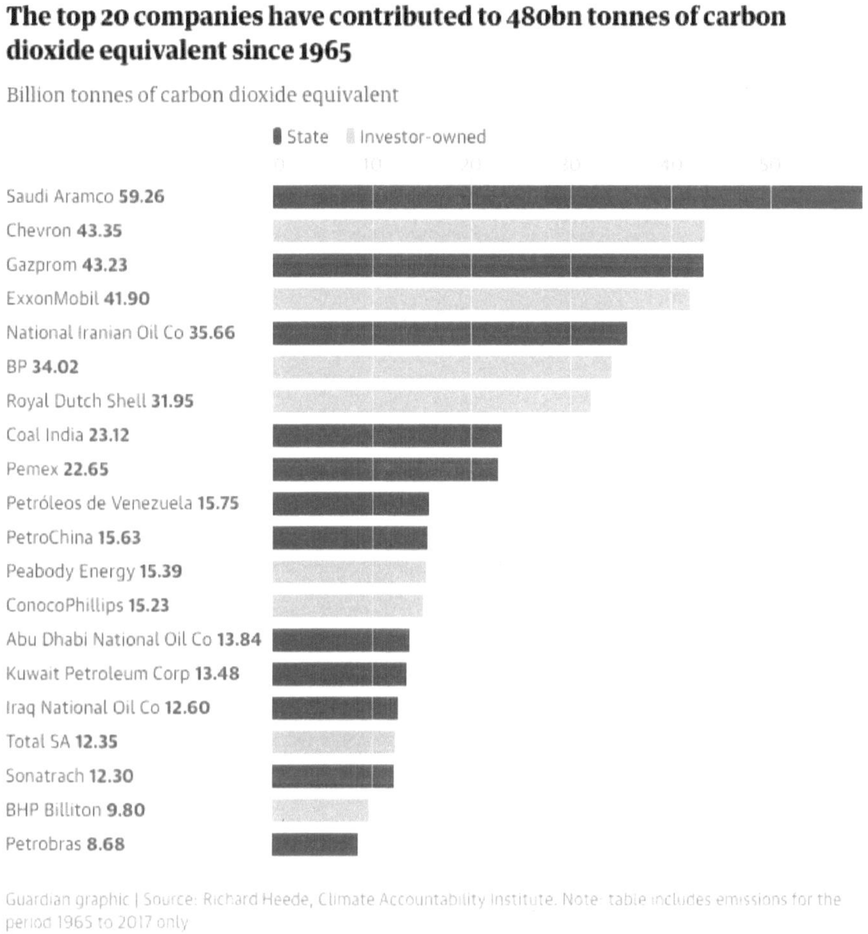

The top 20 companies have contributed to 480bn tonnes of carbon dioxide equivalent since 1965

Billion tonnes of carbon dioxide equivalent

Guardian graphic | Source: Richard Heede, Climate Accountability Institute. Note: table includes emissions for the period 1965 to 2017 only

The same article in the Guardian listed the extent of CO2 emissions for which 20 major organizations are collectively responsible. These organizations contributed 480 billion tons of CO2 equivalents since 1965 which amount to 35% of all energy related CO2 and methane worldwide since 1965. It would be interesting to note that this author in 1988 was President of the "International Association of Energy Economics" (IAEE), a professional body which had the chief economists of major coal and oil companies as well as academics and researchers working on energy issues. In the annual address delivered by the President of the IAEE in Luxemburg on July 4-7, 1988, this author surprised the participants at the annual meeting of the IAEE with an issue that was remote from their objectives and generally neglected by the fossil fuel industry. A relevant part of the speech delivered by this author is shown in Annexure I of this volume.

If Villages Perish, India Perishes

A good model to study and discuss is the *Agra –Mathura* trapezium which represents an area of 10,400 square kilometres and covers parts of *Uttar Pradesh and Rajasthan*. The major centers covered under the trapezium are: 1. *Mathura and Vrindavan* towards its northwest corner, 2. *Firozabad* at the southeast corner, 3. *Keoladeo National Park, Bharatpur*, which is in the westwardly direction, and 4. *Agra* which can be considered as the epicentre of this trapezium. Significantly, this region is home to over 40 protected monuments three of which are listed as world heritage sites, namely the Taj Mahal, the *Agra* Fort and *Fatehpur Sikri*. The Taj Mahal, of course, is also one of the Seven Wonders of the World.

The issue that needs to be considered is whether this entire region, which would provide significant benefits from all round development, has really been treated as an integrated complex particularly from the point of view of tourism that has very high potential in the area. Tourist arrivals in 2013 were a total of approximately 4.7 million. In actual fact, among foreign tourists to the *Agra-Mathura* Trapezium, it was well under 2 million that visited this region in the year 2017. This, of course, was larger than the number received in 2013 of 1.55 million foreign tourists. The reason why the whole region itself would benefit greatly from tourism is because even in terms of the supply of agricultural products, vegetables, poultry products, and other edibles the surrounding areas and villages would benefit greatly with an expanded market in *Agra* as well as in *Mathura*.

There is, of course, a serious air pollution problem which is the result of a number of diesel generating sets, which come into being in the cities and suburbs, essentially because the electricity supply is not satisfactory. There is also the problem of sulphur dioxide concentration, which can have a terribly corrosive effect on the Taj Mahal itself. Fortunately, the NO2 levels are, by and large, within standards except for a few measurements around the Taj Mahal. There is also a serious water pollution problem and this is particularly relevant to the *Yamuna* River and, of course, in the drinking water supply as well as in the domestic waste water treatment provisions. The major source of waste water in *Agra* is the city sewage. Organized industries generally have their own treatment facilities. However, there are a large number of unregistered units which are placed throughout the city. Hence, one of the major improvements that would have to be brought about in the *Agra-Mathura-Firozabad* region is an improvement both in water quality and air quality. In the absence of actions to bring about such improvements, there would be a sharp deterioration in some of the world heritage sites which are located in the region, and a loss of income on account of reduced tourism.

Overall, the tourism trade in *Agra* and *Mathura* is nowhere near satisfactory levels. There has essentially been stagnation in the number of tourists visiting *Agra* and there is a decline in average period of stay. This clearly is a major source of reduced inflow of revenues and resources for the region. Most tourists end up spending a very short average period of stay and as a result the occupancy levels of hotels has come down sharply and so have other associated business opportunities essentially linked with the tourism trade.

There are a large number of problems related to the poor quality of air in the region. These are essentially related to unsatisfactory supply of electric power, major transportation and traffic issues, the location of small scale industries, not necessarily in *Agra* itself, but in the surrounding areas, some small scale industries in *Firozabad*, operation of the *Mathura* Refinery, and greening of the area within the trapezium itself. Each of these is an issue that would have to be tackled at the local level in the surrounding areas and this is where local accountability and decision making capabilities would have to be ensured in the region as a whole, because these are issues which cannot be pushed top downwards.

As far as water pollution is concerned, *Agra* has no sewage treatment facility, and presently a little more than 30% of the city sewage is discharged into old drains. The majority of the population have their own septic tanks or they discharge effluents into various local ponds. Within the seven drainage districts in *Agra*, a total area of 3054 hectares is covered by existing drains and the remaining area of 3,053 hectares does not have any drainage system. Another reason for water pollution is the sludge generated in a waterworks facility where the *Yamuna* water is treated for drinking water supply. Sludge produced in the clari-floculators in the treatment plant and the filter backwash water is being discharged into the River *Yamuna*, through a waste water drain, without any treatment. Sadly, there is also inadequate drinking water supply in the region, including in parts of *Agra* city, and there are, in general, poor sanitation facilities, which clearly have a direct impact on underground water resources. The pattern of unsustainable development in *Agra* and *Mathura*, the two major urban centers, has serious impacts on the adjoining rural areas as well particularly in respect of air and water pollution and the adequacy of water supply.

While it is not the intention to deal with each of the solutions required in the trapezium area, it is important to remember that *Agra* has experienced a continuous setback to the tourism trade, particularly in relation to what the potential for this enormously rare complex is capable of achieving. Some of the reasons why there has been a stagnation in tourists, particularly foreign tourist inflows, coming to *Agra* and to some extent to *Mathura* is the result of : (1) low average duration of stay of tourists in *Agra*, which is presently under one night; (2) chaotic traffic conditions and inadequate local transport facilities; (3) no evening entertainment which forces tourists to remain confined to their hotels or avoid spending the night at *Agra*; (4) over-selling of only the Taj Mahal, *Agra* Fort and *Fatehpur Sikri*; (5) menace of hawkers; (6) lack of an appropriate information center and related facilities; (7) lack of public conveniences and rest places at the monuments and in the city; (8) inadequate maintenance of monuments; and (9) poor hygienic condition of the city, etc. It is obvious that many of the initiatives that are required to create equitable and balanced development of the region are initiatives that have to be taken within the towns and cities themselves. There is a need, therefore, of ensuring that the linkages between rural areas and the supply that they would be able to provide to the cities are clearly established and the number of tourists and the nights they spend in *Agra* is substantially enhanced.

In defining the relationship between cities and villages Gandhi in fact wanted that, "In the state of the future, it will subserve the villages and their crafts. Nothing will be allowed to be produced by the cities that can equally well be produced by the villages. The proper function of the cities is to serve as clearing houses for village products."

The reason why this simple example is being provided is only to show that while there has been rapid growth of urban areas in the country, there is still very poor level of expertise and initiatives by which these urban areas themselves are really being developed effectively quite apart from integration of surrounding rural areas in coordination. The point also that needs to be made is that if there was an understanding of marketing linkages between rural areas and the cities, then much employment could be generated in rural areas themselves, and there would really be no need for those unemployed in the villages to move into towns and cities and create slums with a total lack of conveniences and facilities. Hence, in view of what Gandhiji advocated, there is a need to ensure that rural areas have the wherewithal, the right levels of expertise, and the accountability to ensure local government by which development can take place in a balanced manner. If that were to happen, and if this was to fall within the overall framework of a regional approach, then obviously there would be benefits all around, not only to urban residents, but also to rural areas which could effectively be linked with urban activity all around.

There is a need for micro-level initiatives which would be based on suitable capacity and expertise being created at the level of the *panchayat*, Gandhi's favorite institution for decision-making at the grassroots level in villages. However, based on the approach outlined above, there is clearly a need for coordination on a regional basis, so that villages, as reasonably autonomous units, do not lose benefits of linkages with their surroundings. Gandhi rightly said, "I do not want my house to be walled in on all sides and my windows to be stuffed. I want the cultures of all the lands to be blown about my house as freely as possible. But I refuse to be blown off my feet by any. I refuse to live in other people's houses as an interloper, a beggar, or a slave."

In other words, Gandhi was open to all kinds of influences but did not wish to lose his own identity. Nor did he want the village as a unit to lose its own character. There are cabinet positions in most governments which differentiate between urban development and rural development. In terms of the power and resources that both of these ministries wield, the Urban Development Ministry generally succeeds, not only in terms of budgetary resources, but also in respect of organizational strengths and human resources. At the same time, as is the case with most government departments, ministries function in silos and seldom coordinate their efforts. It is, therefore, essential that we bring about coordination at the local level which clearly lays down specific goals for rural areas as integral to the development of a region as a whole including, where necessary, the development of an urban center. Ideally, at the local level, all those involved in decision-making on development must come together and establish plans which can be implemented on a decentralized basis, but clearly with a close degree of coordination.

In a letter that Gandhi wrote to Nehru in 1945, before the latter became Prime Minister of India, he stated, "My village today lives in my imagination.… He (villager) will not lead his life like an animal in a squalid dark room. Men and women will live freely and be prepared to face the whole world. The villages will not know cholera, plague, or smallpox. No one will live indolently nor luxuriously. After all this, I think of many things which will have to be produced on large scale. I want the two of us (Gandhi and Nehru) to understand each other well."

The example provided above of the *Agra-Mathura* Trapezium would be applicable to many other locations in the world where there is a synergy between urban as well as rural areas contiguous to each other. This is particularly relevant in those cases where tourist income and activities are the dominant economic drivers. A good example would be the region of *Merida* in Mexico, which the Government of Mexico and the local government are trying to develop as a major tourist destination. Clearly, while there are separate municipalities stretch over this region, coordination between them becomes absolutely essential.

A Cooperative Dairy, Primary and Secondary Schools

With increased population density not only of urban locations, but also rural areas, it would be futile to plan for a community in isolation of the rest of the environment. Indeed, as Gandhiji intended, it is necessary to provide adequate governance and accountability to local bodies with expertise that is necessary in today's context. There is, therefore, a need for ensuring proper and continuous coordination between decision-making entities which are contiguous and inter-dependent.

The case in point lies in the terrible air quality in the National Capital Region (NCR) including Delhi and surrounding areas. There are various factors which account for the totally unacceptable quality of air in the NCR, but to this during certain seasons can be added the terrible impact of burning of agricultural residue in the states of *Punjab and Haryana*. Much of the pollution created by this burning traverses to *Delhi* and only adds to the poor air quality in the NCR. The answer obviously lies in a coordinated effort extending over a large area. It is sad that the states and local bodies, which could effectively curb the burning of agricultural residue, have proved ineffective in doing so. This author presented the option of gasification of biomass using agricultural residue as a fuel to the highest authority in *Punjab* in 2014, when the problem was not even so acute. Not only would a set of policies, incentives, and facilitation have helped in curbing air pollution, which obviously affects the people of *Punjab* as well, but it would have provided a useful resource for generating energy on a decentralized basis. In this age of focused expertise, there is, therefore, a growing need for coordinated action among contiguous administrative units by which common objectives could be met through collective and coordinated action.

The case study described earlier focused on the entire region known as *Agra - Mathura* Trapezium. It is truly sad and disappointing that not only does *Agra* contain one of the seven wonders of the world, but also houses many of UNESCO's world heritage sites. Similarly, *Mathura* is a destination of pilgrims and those belonging to the Hindu faith who would like to travel to the birth place of Lord *Krishna*. Yet, the facilities in both these towns, in complete isolation of developments of locations from the surrounding areas, have led not only to a completely unsustainable and unconnected form of development, but have as a result compromised on the capacity and unique attractions of *Agra* and *Mathura* for ensuring the inflow of a substantial number of tourists.

While it may be much too complex to get into some of the institutional arrangements by which a reorientation of development plans, priorities, and values can be brought about, what is proposed in this chapter is a complete shift, a possible tectonic shift, not only in respect of the definition of what constitutes development, but also a creation of the capacity at every level of the government by which the objectives enshrined in Gandhian thinking can be constructed as rapidly as possible. What is proposed is a range of activities by which human society can certainly ensure that we mount some programs that can bring about the development of rural areas in a manner that provides a level playing field to all those who live in these locations.

One important component that perhaps needs to be considered is a plan for social entrepreneurs designated for rural areas, who would certainly be able to live at least for a period of three years in rural locations at the end of which if they prefer they can stay on in what might turn out to be a far more pleasant and facilitating environment in these locations and certainly, a much more satisfying career, for those who get involved in social entrepreneurship. There have been a number of initiatives which mobilized expertise and knowledge in the past in several parts of the world. Chairman Mao introduced the "the great leap forward" requiring Chinese villages to set up industrial units, including pig iron furnaces, most of which were a failure. But perhaps that brought in a spirit of enterprise and familiarity with modern technology as an outcome. At the international level, President Kennedy's Peace Corps in the 1960s was generally a successful program with dedicated personnel who brought a high level of expertise in development activities.

There are three specific reasons why it is important to bring about a major reorientation of development policies, not only across the entire world, but certainly in the case of those countries which are seen as developing.

The first reason is that for the past several decades we have seen a complete neglect of activities and development plans related to rural areas. The main emphasis has been on promoting infrastructure and facilities, essentially to expand urban locations, even in countries where population growth has stabilized and has actually not been rising as in some other countries of the world. This means that urban growth is taking place on account of migration from rural areas apart from those coming from other countries.

The second reason is that we really need to focus on what has been termed before as regrowth. There was an urban-centered pattern of growth and development that emerged from industrialization and that lasted at least a century and a half, with, of course, several modifications and through the process of technological evolution which has taken place over time. But this has essentially created a monolith of industrial and human activities across the entire globe. What we need to do now is to ensure that grow is equitable and sustainable and can assist and provide a fair set of opportunities to the poorest of the poor, who in most areas, particularly in the developing world, live in rural locations. As mentioned earlier, even in China, where perhaps 700 – 800 million people have been lifted out of poverty in the past five years, or so, the rural population has become poorer. This is essentially due to a bias in promoting urbanization and the allocation of resources in favor of towns and cities at the cost of rural areas.

The third reason why it is crucially important for us to reorient development policies is because urbanization chokes the ability of urban dwellers to get anywhere close to nature and this has major implications for the Gandhian view of life which, clearly combines not only physical and mental wellbeing of every individual with his or her aspirations, but also makes sure that there is a spiritual component in a person's development. Nature imbues a human being with a cheerful personality as well as a sense of hope and oneness with nature which is essential for optimism that it inspires. It is particularly important that the reversal of decline in natural resources and their stock must take place urgently. Reversal is also needed related to the decline in the ability of human society to identify with nature which has clearly been eroded over time. It is essential for us to restore as rapidly as possible the kinds of access that existed earlier in terms of getting close to nature.

This, the final point, is crucially important because it defines the very nature of the Gandhian view of development and a view that now needs to be revived and resuscitated because we are clearly at a stage where the excess of materialism that human beings are pursuing today and the enormous amount of waste which we are generating certainly detracts from what constitutes human happiness.

****

Leaning on Gandhi's vision for energy access planning and integrated rural development

by

Dr. Shonali Pachauri

About two-third of India's population still resides in its villages in relatively primitive conditions. Energy is vital for development and for improving living conditions and yet access to modern energy services and other basic infrastructure is still far from universal for these populations. In April 2018, the Government of India declared that every single village of India has access to electricity. However, the reality is much more complex.

Official data deems a village electrified if power cables from the grid reach a transformer in each village and 10% of its households, as well as public places such as schools and health centers, are connected. This indicator says nothing about the quality of electric supply or the services that the supply power or how that benefits the people using it. Recent research shows that millions of households and small rural businesses remain without grid electricity access despite official claims that 100% household access has been achieved by India in January 2019 (SPI& ISEP 2019). Furthermore, two of every five rural households are dissatisfied with the electricity service they receive from public utilities according to recent surveys (SPI& ISEP 2019).

Dissatisfaction with the pace of rural electrification and quality of energy and other basic services supplied to rural consumers has resulted in a redoubling of efforts for decentralized energy supply for sustainable rural development, and to involve local stakeholders, build local capacity to develop and manage infrastructure locally. These efforts are in line with

Gandhi's view of decentralization, self-sufficiency, and integrated rural development. Mahatma Gandhi's concept of 'back to the village' resonates even today particularly with global goals to increase equity – leave no one behind - and calls for further democratization of societies. Gandhi sought to develop India from the bottom with a focus on the poorest and the weakest. He emphasized the centrality of the village. He believed that a strengthened and sound rural economy could revitalize the nation and small communities molding their lives and planning their own development based on voluntary cooperation were the best means to avoid exploitation, poverty, and unemployment. Self-sufficient villages, producing mostly for their own consumption, was the way to a peaceful life and pursuit of democratic values according to Gandhi.

Efforts at decentralized modes of electrification have also gained traction in recent years because of the challenges with grid extension in many poor rural areas where low population densities and vast transmission distances result in high marginal costs of connection relative to expected demand. Decentralized efforts are seen as a way to overcome some of the challenges of centralized capital-intensive infrastructures allowing for more diffuse and community-based efforts that maybe more democratic. However, how decentralized efforts are organized and implemented appear to have a significant bearing on the stream of benefits that flow from these (GNESD 2015; WRI 2017). Inadequate planning for and implementation of decentralized off-grid and mini-grid projects has been associated with inadequate provision of energy services to meet required needs and poor maintenance of infrastructure and systems.

Enhancing human welfare and enabling development requires a range of energy services from the most basic domestic uses, such as illumination and cooking, to more sophisticated ones such as refrigerated cooling, thermal comfort and entertainment, as well as productive, transport, and community applications. While physical availability provides a simple metric for capturing one dimension of access, it ignores several other dimensions or attributes associated with access and leaves room for ambiguity as regards the spatial scale at which access is defined (for example, at a community level, household, or individual level). Other important dimensions of access include acceptability and convenience, adequacy, affordability, reliability, safety, legality, efficiency, and service quality (the multidimensionality of energy access has been discussed by Pachauri 2011; Pachauri and Spreng 2011, Practical Action 2012, WB GTF 2013, Pelz & Pachauri 2018, etc.).

Options and technologies for improving access are manifold and encompass different scales and purposes. For electrification, options range from centralized grid-based systems to smaller micro-grids and modular off-grid technologies using either fossil fuels or renewables. For cooking, the options are equally diverse from improved stoves that use traditional solid fuels, to those that use processed biomass (pellets, biogas, ethanol, etc.), cleaner-combusting fossil fuels such as Liquified Petroleum Gas (LPG) and natural gas or even electricity. For transportation, options include both public and private modes powered by petrol and diesel, compressed natural gas, newer bio-based fuels, or even electricity. Finally, mechanical power solutions range from diesel powered engines to wind and watermills and other renewable and fossil energy powered motors.

In India, early rural electrification efforts, post-independence, were motivated by providing cheap power to farmers for irrigation pumping. As a consequence, electrification occurred through expansion of the central grid in the fertile wheat growing states. But often the poorest communities were skipped over and the extremely low tariff structures for farmers and households that were put in place then had consequences for the future profitability of the state owned electricity utilities and had severe environmental consequences (Dubash& Rajan 2001). While the green revolution that was brought about in part by intensification of irrigation increased food security and brought benefits to many people in India, the benefits of electrification accrued to a relative few. Even after more than seven decades of Indian independence, unfortunately, rural electrification has not directly benefited most of the rural population. Experience has shown that, beyond the obvious uses of electricity for lighting, radios, and basic home-appliances, the uses of electricity for purposes that might improve livelihoods and bring development to an area are slow to emerge without institutional mechanisms in place conducive to fostering entrepreneurial activity and productive uses of electricity (Pachauri & Spreng 2013).

Recent visions of "smart villages" where community efforts are integrated with information and communication technologies to provide benefits to rural communities can be viewed as new interpretations of Gandhi's vision (Somwanshi et al. 2016). A smart village is envisioned as one in which modern energy access acts as a catalyst for development in education, health, security, productive enterprises, and the environment. The emphasis is on improved resource use efficiency, local self-governance, assured access to basic amenities, and responsible individual and community behavior to build happy societies. Similar calls for more integrated and equitable approaches to energy and infrastructure development are also enshrined in the United Nations Sustainable Development Agenda 2030.

****

We have probably not learnt any useful lessons from the neglect of rural areas in the past because even when we are implementing modern technology on a large scale across the country, we seem to neglect what benefits should rightly and in a fair manner accrue to our rural population. On the 17th of October 2019, BBC came up with an interesting assessment of the fact that while India has more than 630 million internet subscribers, for every Indian who has access to the internet there is at least one who does not, and that person is most likely living in a rural area. What this report says is that if you look at the rural population, which is around 66%, the internet density is barely 25.3 %, whereas the urban population which constitutes 34% of the total, has an internet density of 97.9 %. This clearly is something which needs to be corrected and there has to be an intelligent approach by which rural persons can also receive the benefits of modern technology and connectivity which is going to be crucially important for the development of these regions. As it happens, there are mountainous areas in *Himachal Pradesh, Uttarkahand* and those even in the *Darjeeling* Hills, as also the deserts of *Rajasthan* and the tribal regions in *Madhya Pradesh* which are completely excluded from the so-called digital revolution. Yet, these are the very communities which need to be connected in a manner such that they do not continue or multiply with the terrible disadvantages that they have been suffering from in the past. It was also reported that only 16% of Indian women were found to be using mobile and internet services, which clearly brings out the gender divide in Indian society.

When it comes to social entrepreneurs, there are some interesting innovations which have been tried. For instance in the case of *Bihar*, the government has set up a so called NGO called *Jeevika*, which has done quite remarkable work in a number of fields as a kind of development agency functioning in rural areas. But it is also in some respects a bureaucratic entity where the structure at the top consists only of government officials. And, therefore, the means by which implementation of programs takes place is often plagued by bureaucratic procedures and systems. What would be extremely effective in most rural locations would be an organization which is structured broadly and which could very well be statewide. But an effective structure should be such that not only would government officials guide the destiny of the organization, but a number of other experts and those who are altruistically inclined should be able to help rural populations in a variety of ways including, of course, modern systems of connectivity. There would also be some merit in the government providing support for connectivity for which they would need to pursue in an effective and measurable way. This, of course, raises the whole issue of the kinds of metrics and measures by which social entrepreneurship needs to be evaluated and assessed. This clearly requires intellectual efforts which must be embedded in local government at the *panchayat* level so that any program that is scrutinized is not merely left to the government at the state level or the government at the central level. While these agencies really have a definite role to play, particularly where government funds and sanctions have to be considered, what would be particularly important is to empower and create capacity within the *panchayats* at the local government level itself.

One extremely important omission, particularly as it relates to Gandhi's concept of rural development, has been the lack of growth of the cooperative movement in India. This is a subject which needs to be considered very carefully. Given particularly the importance of what Dr Verghese Kurien was able to achieve with the Operation Flood program. Miraculously milk production in India increased by leaps and bounds essentially on the strength of the cooperative movement, which also brought prosperity to rural populations in a remarkable way.

Hence, one very useful institutional arrangement that could address some of the disparities between the poorest people living in rural areas and rich landholders and an arrangement which is essentially market oriented, is the cooperative movement. The International Labor Office (ILO) in Geneva brought out, some years, ago a useful paper entitled "The Role of Cooperatives in achieving the Sustainable Development Goals – the Economic Dimensions." This paper starts by mentioning the fact that there are 2.6 million cooperative societies and since that time in 2014, when the paper was published, perhaps the number would have grown significantly. It also mentions that there are over one billion members of these cooperative societies and it has a combined turnover of three trillion US Dollars. It goes on to say that the global cooperative movement is the largest organization in the world, bigger in terms of its membership than the trade union movement, and economically more powerful then several G20 countries. It provides employment to many more people then all multinational companies taken together. Hence, in theory such an important movement should be central to the international development agenda. Yet, despite its size and power, the movement has not been very influential in the post-2005 debate.

The cooperative movement, in several parts of the world, is constrained by major limitations of rules regulations and legislations. An example of this can be found in the cooperative movement in India which essentially carries the provision of a District Officer, essentially a bureaucrat, who can dissolve a cooperative based on what he perceives may be a deviation from the rules that the cooperative is obliged to follow. This may be very valid in some cases, but essentially if the cooperative itself has a bottom upwards approach then it has the power of the people which certainly provides large benefits to the people who are members and to society at large. An excellent example of the cooperative movement lies in what has been called the white revolution in India, a major innovation using the cooperative structure, which Dr. Verghese Kurien, a genius in every respect, and indefatigable champion of cooperatives and those who are its members, has been able to achieve. It would be useful to follow the write up which is still maintained as a record of Dr. Kurien's various achievements. Unfortunately, he died several years ago and while this was an individual who should have won the Nobel Peace Prize for what he was able to accomplish and bring into existence against all odds. He essentially passed away not even being acknowledged by the Government of India for the highest honour in the land, which is called the *Bharat Ratna*. In a very modest tribute to Dr. Kurien, words which his website carries are provided below:

"Operation Flood started the White Revolution in India and made our country self-sufficient in milk and this was achieved entirely through the cooperative structure. Today around 12 million farmers, in more than 22 states across the country, own around 250 dairy plants handling around 20 million litres of milk a day. This is a remarkable achievement. While we, in India, tend to take our achievement for granted, this feat elicited high praise and admiration throughout the world."

"In 1955, our butter imports were 500 tons per year; today our cooperatives alone produce more than 12,000 tons of butter. Similarly, we imported 3,000 tons of baby food in 1955; today our cooperatives alone produce 38,000 tons of baby food. By 1975, all imports of milk and milk products stopped. The import permitted was that of food aid under Operation Flood."

"A separate agency, called as the Indian Dairy Corporation (IDC), was created to receive grants of food aid and use it in Operation Flood. This agency was also headed by the marvelous Dr. Verghese Kurien." "Milk powder production increased from 22,000 tons in the pre-Operational Flood year to 1,40,000 tons by 1989."

Cooperatives are perhaps the ideal arrangement for a diverse range of produce emanating from agricultural and other activities in rural areas. However, in several parts of the world, most notably, India where we have a number of people still connected with agricultural, horticultural, and livestock related activities, cooperatives have not really been spread nor have they been effective in terms of the constraints that they are subjected to. The ILO paper, very rightly summarizes, several of the challenges of the cooperative model. These include for instance:

1. The challenge of the environment where it states that in some coun-

tries cooperative policies, cooperative laws, and cooperative support institutions are still not fully conducive to the emergence and proper functioning of genuine, democratically controlled, and economically viable cooperatives. Even though it states that substantial progress has been made in the areas since the mid-1990s, in some cases, liberalization may have gone too far and exposed members to fraud. In the case of India, unfortunately, it is the restrictions and regulations that govern the formation and more importantly, the operation of cooperatives, which have been a major handicap in their growth. This is something that Dr. Kurien expressed on several occasions where he felt that the power of the people and the ability for people to exercise their choices through cooperative movements are often hampered by antiquated laws and regulations which clearly restrict their functioning.

2. The challenge of size is another issue that clearly hampers the growth of cooperatives. These entities need to be big enough to reach the economic breakeven point and small enough to allow individual members to meaningfully participate. This publication suggests that the optimal size of a cooperative is, therefore, dictated by economic factors –financial cooperatives may reach the breakeven point earlier than for instance marketing cooperatives - as well as social and societal factors. It states that the latter also explains why cooperatives are more successful in certain African communities then in others. In the case of India apparently, cooperatives have been uniquely successful in the state of Gujarat although in some other parts of the country they have not always functioned effectively. This clearly means that we have not spent enough intellectual capital to understand and optimize the development and functioning of cooperatives across the world. If power is provided to the members of cooperatives, in rural areas for instance, this would accord very closely with Gandhi's concept of decentralized governance and, therefore, we really need to understand and conceptualize the types of cooperatives that might be useful under specific economic and social conditions in various countries and communities.

3. There is, of course, the challenge of management, where cooperative

members are consumers, farmers, workers, and fisherman, as well as informal economy operators, artisans etc. Of course, one cannot expect these members to become managers and yet, smaller cooperatives cannot afford to hire professional managers and, therefore, need to rely on skills of elected leaders who may excel in the trade but have never seen a balance sheet. In this respect the social entrepreneurs who have been described above could very well be associated with cooperatives and provide the management and related expertise to cooperatives particularly in their formative stages. Subsequently, when these cooperatives grow there would be perhaps enough justification for them to hire professional managers. This has certainly happened with the white revolution where Amul, for instance, the brand that is produced by the milk cooperative in several parts of India, competes effectively with even the international and multinational organizations which promote their own well-known brands. The level of innovation inherent in the management of Amul has proved far more powerful and far more competitive then several other brands which are not only available in India but have been successful all over the world.

4. There is also the challenge of innovation because the observation is that cooperatives have been far more widespread in the case of traditional sectors of national economies such as commercial agriculture, retail distribution and finance. However, modern economic systems which are now internet-based require new forms of cooperatives. One can see why brands such as Amazon have been so successful because they have utilized the power of the internet as well as the economies of scale that would make it possible for such a company to become almost a universal source of various products and services that can be provided.

5. The challenge of flexibility is also important because the Sustainable Development Goals (SDGs) require cooperation, but not necessarily, formally registered fully-fledged cooperatives. Cooperatives must stay true to their values while adjusting to the realities of a changing world. Overall, therefore, it is crucially important that we study the successes and failures of cooperatives across the world and at the same time

anticipate some of the challenges they would need to face, particularly with the development of technology of various kinds. And of course the spread of cooperatives in different parts of the world would also require partnership with governments and, in fact, these have to be initiated by governments because of the regulatory, institutional, and legislative initiatives that would be required.

Another remarkable organization based on the cooperative system is known as IFFCO, the Indian Farmers Fertilizer Cooperative Limited This was an organization established by its first Managing Director, Mr. Paul Pothan in 1967. It is, therefore, more than 50 years old now. IFFCO, started on a very modest scale, but has now become a gigantic organization with a number of facilities several subsidiaries including, what is called, the Tokyo General Insurance Company There are subsidiaries such as Indian Potash Limited and *Kisan* Rural Finance Limited among others. The word *Kisan* in Hindi stands for farmer. There is a whole range of entities that are part of IFFCO under its umbrella. There is, for instance, the Jordan India Fertilizer Company and a facility that has been established in Oman. So IFFCO is really a remarkable example of how the cooperative movement can make a difference to a large number of people.

Just to provide an example, if we look at the number of organizations that are affiliated with IFFCO, the number has now reached a total of 55 million farmers in India. It started with a modest membership of 57 cooperatives and today the number of cooperative members is more than 36,000. The turnover of IFFCO in 2018-19 was a total of almost 28,000 crores (almost 4.0 billion USD) and it generated a healthy profit before tax of almost 1,160 crores (approximately 164 million USD). In terms of net worth, the cooperative attained a total net worth of 16,269.48 crores (about 2.30 billion USD). So this is in every respect a gigantic enterprise which has clearly been of enormous benefit to India are most valuable is its benefits to such a large number of farmers. IFFCO is now diversifying and providing a whole range of services to the farming community. This can prove to be a major model, not only for other parts of India, which are not covered by IFFCO and its major spread, but also for other parts of the world. In particular, the IFFCO model would be extremely useful for countries of Africa which are attempting to improve their agriculture. In terms of the major challenge that African nations face on account of a rising population, it is important to see that every farmer on that continent benefits from a model organization which has been uniquely successful in India with an essential grassroots presence and the involvement of a very large number of farmers.

The critical feature of a cooperative of this nature is that once it attains a certain size and reaches certain economies of scale, it is able to harness expertise and provide professional inputs which naturally a small cooperative or any sub-optimal entity would not be able to mobilize or afford. IFFCO is also a part of a global network of fertilizer organizations which is headquartered in Paris, known as the International Fertilizer Association. It, therefore, also has the benefit of looking at global practices and global challenges which are related to a vision of the future. One of the areas that is particularly important for the IFA is the whole issue of climate change and how agriculture and the use of fertilizers and the manner in which this set of inputs would evolve in the future would be able to tackle the challenge of climate change.

All in all, cooperatives would be a very direct and appropriate answer to Gandhi's philosophy of promoting rural development and keeping people in villages with a number of opportunities and economic potential which would, not only reduce the disparities between urban and rural dwellers, but also promote the welfare of people who are essentially totally deprived and removed from the current stage of development in many countries.

By implication, Gandhi must have found great merit in the institutional arrangements for cooperatives which could perhaps implement his vision of villages. Cooperatives, by their very definition, are not necessarily dictated to by government at higher levels but are essentially managed by human beings who become part of a particular cooperative. His view on this was, "Only a radical change will do. An end to little holdings and introduction of organized collective farms and cooperative enterprises. The land will not and cannot absorb all our people – and others must turn to small-scale industry, but in the main, to large-scale socialized industries and social services. These thoughts brought nearer each other the middle class, the intelligentsia and the peasants. The adoption of the simple white *khadi* dress by the middle class resulted in simplicity and a feeling of unity with the masses. Even the poorest felt something of this dignity and self-respect."

These words are truly profound, because firstly they emphasize the need for a radical change. Such a change is what is being advocated in this book in the form of what one could describe as a tectonic shift, simply because the environmental and ecological problems facing the planet require a radical and substantial shift to Gandhian philosophy. Gandhi also emphasized the need for cooperative enterprises, which have remained stillborn in several parts of the world, most notably in India, the land which calls Gandhi the Father of the Nation. He also saw the need for the land not being able to absorb all the people in agricultural professions and, therefore, the development of small scale industry and a linkage with large scale socialized industries and social services. This would involve coordinated planning and action with urban centers as part of contiguous rural locations. With these words he also emphasized the need for middle class intelligentsia and the peasants. Such a view would support the need for social entrepreneurs and possibly a much larger region-based approach that doesn't necessarily focus on urban areas, but also the hinterland of rural locations and surroundings which must be integrated with what Gandhi calls the "large-scale socialized industries and social services". We, therefore, need to ensure that the radical shift that Gandhi has talked about is implemented as rapidly as possible so that we are able to address some of the chronic ills of society including the environmental, the ecological, and human induced climate change related problems with the issue of growing disparities of income and wealth, which clearly are a result of the form of urbanization which is being followed in most parts of the world.

****

Energy, health, and education
by
Dr. Saroj Pachauri

Health Services

Gandhiji believed that health services should be made available to all. He conceptualized a village-based model of health care and education. In the 1950s, India initiated a program to provide primary health care in rural areas where 80% of the population resided. A vast network of sub-centers, primary health centers, and district hospitals has been established over these years. Millions of frontline workers have been trained to provide health services at the doorstep. As a result of these efforts, mortality and fertility have declined. There is, however, a long way to go because India must not only combat communicable diseases but also address the growing problem of non-communicable diseases including cardiovascular disease, diabetes etc. India is currently bearing a double burden of disease. Achieving universal health care will need much greater, concerted efforts, and innovation.

Would Gandhiji have foreseen this scenario? One can only speculate. But he certainly envisioned health services for the rural poor. The government began by providing health services in rural areas where progress has been made. However, today the plight of the urban poor is far worse than that of the rural poor. Large numbers of poor rural men and women are flocking to the big urban cities for employment and livelihoods resulting in a proliferation of urban slums that are basset with health and social problems. Growing socio-economic disparities is foreseen as a serious problem which will result in unprecedented social upheaval and health crises.

Demographics

The population of India at 1.3 billion, is seen as a major problem, as population is viewed to be outstripping resources. The perception is that it is India's biggest problem. India will not be able to feed, clothe, educate and provide employment and healthcare to these extraordinarily large members of people. Consequently, coercive measures that bely human rights, are the government's frequent knee-jerk reaction for resolving the problem.

On the other hand, women in India, including poor, rural women do not want more than two or three children. The average number of children born to a woman is 2 or less in more than ten states in the country. These states have achieved replacement level fertility. Despite these achievements, however, the numbers of people continue to grow because of population momentum. A large proportion (62.5%) of India's population is young (15 to 49 years of age). Although these young people do not want more than one to two children, India's population will continue to grow. This demographic dividend can be harnessed for India's benefit but only if investments in health and education are made now. If India is successful in this endeavor, healthy young, educated people will be brought into the employment stream to become productive resources for the country thereby, enhancing economic growth and productivity. But providing healthcare and education and generating employment opportunities are essential pre-requisites for achieving this outcome.

<u>Medical Internship: The Najafgarh Experience</u>

After completion of medical studies, we went through a one-year internship period when, by rotation, we were exposed to the various disciplines of medicines. An important part of the internship was a three-month residency in a village. The purpose was to expose the students to the health problems of the rural poor who, at the time comprised 80% of the country's population.

I was an intern in Najafgarh, a rural area outside Delhi. During my rural internship, I participated in a project on sanitary latrines. Recognizing that open defecation was the single most important cause of gastro-intestinal diseases with diarrhea being the most important cause of mortality and morbidity especially in children, the Ford Foundation had funded a project to set up sanitary latrines in rural areas. A survey had been undertaken among the population of Najafgarh to assess whether the people would like to use latrines if these were provided to them free of cost. The survey results had revealed that this rural community was positive to the idea. Consequently, sanitary latrines was constructed in the villagers' homes.

When our batch of medical students was posted in Najafgarh, we were assigned the task of visiting the homes of the villagers to enquire about their experience of using latrines. The results of our survey were shocking. None of the latrines were being used! Everyone including women and children, continued the same old practice of defecating in the fields. It was hypothesized that women, in particular, would find the latrines useful. However, this assumption was completely refuted. The women enjoyed their social outing in the cool of the morning with the breeze blowing through the fields. This was a welcome period for sharing and gossiping. A joyful outing which otherwise was not possible, as women were not permitted to go outside their homes.

As for using the latrines that had been constructed in their homes, it was incomprehensible to everyone…man or woman…that the dirtiest job should be done in the precincts of their home. The obvious question that came to mind which we asked the householders was "Then why did you accept the offer of having the latrine constructed?" The answer was unanimous. "How could we say 'No' when the offer was made so graciously by our guests?"

Thus, the sanitary latrine project undertaken in 1958-59 was a complete failure. But like all failed projects, it provided many important lessons. Have we learned any lessons from that or from subsequent experiences? Millions of latrines are now being constructed under *Swachh Bharat Abhiyaan* (SBA). Will Gandhi's dream of *swachh bharat* be realized? Gandhi had himself provided a personal example of cleaning his own latrine and also compelling his wife, *Kasturba* to do so since he envisioned Sewagram as a model village. Gandhiji remarked "if we do not keep our backyards clean, our Swaraj (Freedom) will have a fowl strench."

Swachh Bharat Abhiyaan (SBA) was launched on October 2, 2014, Gandhi's birth anniversary. The aim was to achieve universal sanitation and to make India open defecation free by October 2, 2019, Mahatma Gandhi's 150th anniversary.

The goal was universal sanitation or disposal of waste and bringing an end to open defecation to fulfil Gandhi's dream. Through the world's largest toilet building initiative, SBA, more than 95 million toilets have been constructed across rural and urban India since its launch.

Since this is the final year of the program (October 2, 2019), it is important to examine its outcomes, not only in terms of improved sanitation and defecation free areas, but also in terms of its impact on the outbreak of vector-borne diseases such as dengue, chikungunya and on diarrheal disease outbreaks.

Using data from the National Integrated Surveillance Program, Dandabathula et al., 2019 undertook an analysis of acute diarrheal disease (ADD) outbreaks from 2010 to 2018(1). The number of ADD outbreaks per year in 2017 and 2018 were less than in any previous year. Seasonal variations during May-August account for 55-60% of ADD outbreaks in any year but in the years 2017 and 2018 these were 46%, significantly lower than in other years. Thus, this study shows that SBA had an impact on diarrheal disease.

Socio-economic status and education of the mother are clearly associated with the higher incidence of diarrhea in young children. Poor sanitation and unhygienic conditions are important contributory factors for diarrheal disease. Measures for prevention of diarrheal disease include safe water, hard washing, and safe disposal of excreta among others. Poor sanitation, lack of access to clean water, and poor personal hygiene are responsible for childhood diarrheal diseases in India. Addressing other social determinants including poverty alleviation and educating women are necessary measures for improving overall health and reducing mortality due to diarrhea in children.

Reference:

1.Dandabathula G, Bhardwaj P, Burra M, Rao PVVP, Rao SS. Impact assessment of India's Swachh Bharat Mission - Clean India Campaign on acute diarrheal disease outbreaks: Yes, there is a positive change. J Fam Med Prim Care. 2019 Mar;8(3):1202–8.

Gandhiji: Some Reflections

My earliest memory of Gandhi is when I was five or six years old. We lived in *Rawalpindi* (Pindi) in a house within the campus of the District Hospital where my mother worked. In-charge of the women's section of the hospital, she was one of two women doctors in the district. My mother, *Dr. Basant Kumari* was the only government women doctor; the second, *Dr. Shakuntala* was a private practitioner.

Beyond the boundary wall of our house was a road lined by bungalows. When he visited Pindi, Gandhiji stayed in one of those bungalows as a guest of a family who were his loyal devotees. On one such visit, my mother took me along when she went to meet Gandhiji. I recall a rather large room filled with several people, many of whom were women. Gandhiji was very affectionate. He took me in his lap. If only there was a photograph to have captured that very special moment.

My mother Basant *Kumari,* a devotee of Gandhiji, went regularly for his prayer meetings in New Delhi when she was a student of medicine at the Lady Hardinge Medical College. She and some of her like-minded friends went together for these meetings. Prominent among them was *Dr. Susheela Nayyar,* who later devoted herself to the service of Gandhi for as long as he was alive. She is seen in many photographs walking with Gandhiji.

After Gandhi was no more she entered into politics and was appointed Health Minister in the Union Cabinet. In 1939, nestled in the lap of *Sewagram,* she set up the Mahatma Gandhi Institute of Medical Sciences. She remained as Principal of the institute until she died in 2001.

During that period, she visited my mother a few times. Senior students were called *bhainji* (older sister). *Dr. Susheela Nayyar* called my mother *Basant bhainji*. I met her a couple of times when she came to see my mother in New Delhi. In fact, I was myself a medical student at the same medical college where *Basant Kumari* and *Susheela Nayyar* had studied many years earlier.

My mother got married in a village in the *Punjab*. Quite unlike all brides who were decked in silk and adorned with gold jewels, my mother, a true Ghandhian, wore a red *khadi* suit and adorned herself with flowers instead of with gold jewellery.

Gandhiji was assassinated on January 30,1948. I can never forget how my mother wept. I had never seen her cry before this. Mrs. *Sharma*, our neighbor also ran out of her house weeping bitterly. These woman felt that their father had gone, as the Father of the Nation passed away.

Correct for Systemic Distortions Prior to Catastrophic Failures

P hil McDuff, who writes for The Guardian and is clearly a person with a conscience and someone who writes fearlessly on some very basic issues that afflict our society, has actually written an article the thrust of which is very significant. It has a title which goes as follows "Ending climate change requires the end of capitalism. Have we got the stomach for it?" The author rightly says that policy tweaks won't do, we need to throw the kitchen sink at this with a total rethink of our relationship to ownership, work, and capital. He does not quite spell out exactly how the issue of ownership related to work and capital would perhaps function in practice if we were to deal with the growing challenge of climate change.

McDuff refers to the movement, which has been started by the 16-year old Swedish girl, Greta Thunberg, requiring students all over the world to stay out of class and demonstrate for action on climate change. He rightly mentions that today's children, as they become more politically aware, will be much more radical than their parents, simply because there will be no other choice for them. This indeed is true because we know that climate change is going to present much higher risks in the future and those who are either in their teens or early 20s and, of course, those much younger would face severe problems as a result of human induced climate change, something that previous generations have been responsible for. One could even argue that till about the 1980s, there was very little awareness on what causes climate change as a result of human actions, but there is absolutely no excuse or escape from the fact that today we know what the reasons are for climate change and the fact that our persistence with fossil fuels and the pattern of economic growth and development that we have spread all over the world is really playing havoc into the climate system, and therefore, with the lives of the young who are with us today and those who are yet to come in the future.

McDuff feels that right now we can with a massive investment effort by 2030, just about keep the warming level below 1.5°C. He feels this is a bad but manageable territory. However, if we fail to do this, then the world will certainly cross into severe temperature barriers that would lead to outcomes like a collapse of the ecosystems around the world, much higher acidification of the oceans, large-scale desertification, and coastal cities being flooded to a point where they become totally inhabitable.

It might be mentioned that as the Fifth Assessment Report of the IPCC clearly brought out, 30% of the carbon dioxide emitted since the beginning of industrialization has gone into the oceans and this has raised acidification levels to a serious extent, which obviously will have an impact on marine life and marine ecosystems. Further increases in acidification will only make the problem far more acute. McDuff says that we will simply have to throw the kitchen sink at this because policy tweaks like carbon tax will really not do. As stated above, what he suggests is that we should fundamentally reevaluate our relationship to ownership, work, and capital. He believes that the impact of a dramatic reconfiguration of the industrial economy requires similarly large changes in the welfare state. Basic incomes, large scale public works programs— everything has to be on the table to ensure that the oncoming system shocks do not leave vast swathes of the global population starving and destitute. He refers with a great deal of relevance to something that came out of a cartoon from The New Yorker where a suited man sat in a post-apocalyptic landscape is telling his young audience "yes, the planet got destroyed. But for a beautiful moment in time we created a lot of value for shareholders". Unfortunately, this depicts exactly what is wrong with our system where shareholders, who have been at the beck and call of the current economic system, have benefitted in several cases, but have left the rest of the population completely deprived of the very basics of existence that might provide human beings at least a dignified form of living in various parts of the world.

McDuff states that many of today's climate strikers, inspired and led by Greta Thunberg, won't even be 30 by the time the 1.5°C deadline comes around in 2030. He feels that they are asking us to consider a simple question: Is the future worth more than preserving our reputations? What will our response to them be? A remarkable intellectual, Nicholas Georgescu-Roegen provided a profound piece of advice to economists with his statement, "The point is that for the resources *in situ*, not only the present generations but all future ones, should also bid. And since future generations cannot be present now, we must bid in their place, a point that brings us back to the bioeconomic principle: mankind must not discount the future."

We certainly need to throw the kitchen sink at the current system of economics. But anyone who suggests that we need to go back to Marxist ideology or the practice of communism or for that matter, the implementation of extreme socialist measures, would certainly be off track. We would then not be able to come up with solutions that really improve the lot of even those that they are targeted at, viz. the large number of poor people across the globe. It is in this respect that perhaps what we need is throwing the kitchen sink at the current system and making sure that this sink comes in the shape and form of what Gandhi preached and believed in all his life. Gandhi was rightly critical of the current form of ownership of capital because he certainly required the assumption of trusteeship by the owners of capital who are essentially managing capital on behalf of society at large. He also required that we come up with a more humane system of economic science which focuses essentially on the most deprived and the most underprivileged sections of society.

To some extent, we can look at economic systems such as those prevalent in the Nordic countries or for that matter even an opulent society like that of Switzerland where Gandhi's concept of the *panchayat* really being a form of republic, is seen in what has evolved as the system of Cantons in Switzerland. It is well known that Switzerland is a loosely constructed federal state and the Canton at the very basic grassroots level has the wherewithal for governance, the resources that need to be mobilized to support a large number of activities and a certain level of autonomy that provides freedom to the citizens of a particular Canton. It is well known that Cantons, not only have infrastructure that carries the scale of modernity and technological sophistication, but it also in several cases, has universities and other institutions that thrive and are sought-after by students not only in Switzerland but from several other parts of the world.

What we need urgently, given the seriousness of climate change, is a complete reordering of the system, which McDuff has referred to in terms of ownership, of work, labor and the very basics of what connects all of these together. Most importantly, if we are to introduce a form of Gandhian enlightenment in the current economic system, we will have to make sure that human beings moderate their demands in a manner that clearly reflects externalities imposed, for instance, on the environment and nature, but as also externalities of various other kinds. Such a system would ensure a far more harmonious form of governance as far as natural resources and ecosystems are concerned and also a much more equitable system of government.

Based on the foregoing, it can be seen that to bring about a major structural shift, almost of a tectonic dimension, is absolutely essential if we want to ensure that human society does not develop the flaws that we have been seeing in existence for much too long. It is also essential to ensure that the global commons, particularly the impacts of climate change and the loss of biodiversity and ecosystem services, do not suffer a decline that we have seen in recent decades. Two particular areas deserve some detailed consideration in ensuring that we move as rapidly as possible to a Gandhian pattern of development, particularly as it relates to a growing population of human beings on this planet. It is important to remember what Gandhi said about the question of whether India should become as prosperous as Britain. He was asked whether India wants to reach the same level of prosperity as Britain, to which he responded "how many planets would a country like India require?"

It would be useful to carry out an assessment of what climate change implies and what would be necessary as part of the Paris Agreement on climate change to adhere to the 1.5°C limit, which is now being assessed as perhaps the most desirable outcome by the IPCC in its 2018 Special Report. However, it is important to go back to a Special Report on extreme events and disasters, which was brought out by the IPCC in 2011. This report, in several respects, was a game changer because it moved away from the fallacy of a slow and steady increase in temperatures and warming taking place on a steady and gradual trend in response to human induced climate change. That special report told us in very stark terms that the result of human induced climate change would be an increase in the frequency and intensity of extreme events. The impact of extreme events as well as how these would degrade and destroy the ecosystems of the earth, quite apart from posing a growing hazard to human society, is something that needs to be prevented at all cost. And today we see the disaster and destruction all around us with the growing ferocity of these extreme events.

We would like to refer to the Summary for Policy Makers of the Special Report on 1.5°C, the headline statements of which are provided in Annexure II. Perhaps, it would be useful to provide a brief summary and overview of those headline statements to give us a basis for the difference between a temperature limit of 1.5°C before the end of the century versus 2.0°C, relative to the pre-industrial period. So far human activities have been assessed to cause approximately 1.0°C of global warming above pre-industrial levels. If the current trends continue, then it is likely that we would reach 1.5°C between 2030 and 2052. That clearly means that if there are no additional mitigation measures adopted, then we would certainly exceed 1.5°C by the middle of this century and that may lead us to average temperature increase substantially more than 2°C by the end of the century.

It needs to be specified also that risks related to the impacts of climate change, particularly as they apply to natural and human systems, will be much higher for global warming of 2°C and perhaps lower than those for 1.5°C. There are, of course, various factors by which the magnitude and rate of warming would apply. But there is no getting away from the fact that there would be increasing risks of a disproportionate nature as warming proceeds over a period of time. For instance, the differences between these two levels of temperature increase would be in respect of hot extremes in most inhabited regions, heavy precipitation in several regions and the probability of drought and precipitation deficits in some regions, it may be noted that in some parts of the world, we may even see extreme precipitation events and droughts occurring in the same location. It is also projected that global mean sea level rise will be around 0.1 meter lower with global warming of 1.5°C as compared to 2°C. Of course, the IPCC has warned us long ago that sea level will continue to rise well beyond 2100 and much would depend on the increase in future emission pathways. It is also important to note that a slower rate of sea level rise would enable much greater opportunities for adaptation in the human and ecological systems of small islands, low lying coastal areas, and particularly the deltas, which in several parts of the world contain the largest concentration of population that you find in so-called mega cities on this planet.

It is also projected that species' loss and extinction will be lower at 1.5°C as compared to 2°C. Hence, there would necessarily be lower impacts on terrestrial, freshwater, and coastal ecosystems and this would ensure that we retain more of their services to human society than would be the case otherwise. Limiting global warming to 1.5°C compared to 2°C will also reduce increases in ocean temperature as well as associated increases in ocean acidity and this would decrease ocean oxygen levels. Consequently, limiting temperature increase to 1.5°C by the end of the century is projected to reduce risks to marine biodiversity, fisheries, and ecosystems; their functions and services to humans as illustrated by recent changes to Arctic sea ice and warm water coral reef ecosystems that would also provide far more satisfactory outcomes.

It is also important to look at the projections of climate change related risks to health, livelihoods, global food security, water supply, human security in general, and economic growth. These would certainly increase with global warming of 2°C and would be distinguished further from values associated with 1.5°C. There would be much lower adaptation needs for global warming of 1.5°C compared to 2°C. There are, as was brought out in the Fifth Assessment Report of the IPCC, limits to adaptation and adaptive capacity for some human and natural systems at global warming of 2°C with associated losses. The number and availability of adaptation options vary by sector.

It is now imperative that a Gandhian way of life and development be adopted if we are not to face the disaster of runaway climate change. All pathways that limit global warming to 1.5°C with limited or no overshoot would require the use of carbon dioxide removal (CDR) on the order of 100 to 1,000 gigatons over the 21st century. CDR would be used to compensate for residual emissions and, in most cases, achieve net negative emissions to return global warming to 1.5°C following a peak. CDR deployment of several hundred gigatons of CO_2 is subject to multiple feasibility and sustainability constraints. Estimates of the global emissions outcome of current nationally stated mitigation ambitions as submitted under the Paris Agreement would lead to global greenhouse emissions (GHG) in 2030 of 52-58 gigatons of CO_2 equivalent per year (Gt CO_2 eq. per year) Pathways reflecting these ambitions would not limit global warming to 1.5°C, even if supplemented by very challenging increases in the scale and ambition of emissions reduction after 2030. It is, therefore, urgent and essential that we reduce emissions in the immediate short term. In the Fourth Assessment Report of the IPCC, it was shown that even for limiting temperature increase to around 2°C, we would have to ensure that GHG emissions peak no later than 2020, and these would, therefore, have to come down rapidly thereafter.

Human society has a unique window of opportunity by which we can ensure peaking of emissions no later than 2020 and then a rapid decline such that by 2030 we are able to achieve a pathway on the basis of which we can ensure temperature increase not going beyond 1.5°C by 2040. This would give us a much higher probability of stabilization at that level of 1.5°C if we reach that level by 2040 rather than 2050. In respect of ecosystem services and the benefits that nature provides to human society and all living species, we need to turn to the Summary for Policy Makers from the 2019 assessment by the IPBES. Some headline statements of that report are provided as Annexure III. But it would be useful to review the major thrust of the findings of that particular report.

Firstly, as stated, nature has different concepts for different people including biodiversity, ecosystems, mother earth, systems of life, and other analytical concepts. When it comes to treating Mother Earth as the source of all the services and benefits that all living species receive on planet Earth, we need to look at the ancient belief of the Indigenous people in Latin America, which refers to the earth as *Pacha Mama*. That basically means that the earth is our mother and, therefore, is the fountain of everything that we derive by way of benefits, by way of what gives us life, and what sustains life over a period of time as we move along in life. Both nature and nature's contributions to people are vital for human existence and a good quality of life, which basically entails living in harmony with nature, living in balance and harmony with Mother Earth, and other analytical concepts. While more food, energy and materials than ever before are now being supplied to people in most places, this is increasingly at the expense of nature's ability to provide such contributions in the future. The biosphere, on which humanity is completely dependent, is being altered to an unprecedented level across all spatial scales. Biodiversity – the diversity that defines different species and is spread between species and ecosystems – is declining much faster than at any time in human history.

The assessment puts forward that nature is essential for human existence and good quality of life. Most of nature's contributions to people are not fully replaceable and some, of course, are totally irreplaceable. It is also true that nature's contributions to people are often distributed unequally across space and time and among different segments of society. Human actions are threatening most species with global extinction now more than has been the case in the past. Globally, local varieties and breeds of domesticated plants and animals are disappearing. The loss of diversity, including genetic diversity, poses a serious risk to global food security by undermining the resilience of many agricultural systems to threats such as pests, pathogens, and climate change.

It is also important to point to the management of nature by Indigenous people and local communities which, unfortunately, is under increasing pressure. These communities have a wealth of experience spreading over thousands of years and, therefore, they are totally in tune with what would actually sustain nature and how they might be able to manage it effectively. Nature is essential for achieving the Sustainable Development Goals (SDGs). However, taking into consideration that the SDGs are integrated and indivisible, because that is the manner in which they have been designed, then these need to be implemented nationally. Current negative trends in biodiversity and ecosystems will undermine progress towards 80% which means 35 out of 44 of the assessed targets or goals related to poverty, hunger, health, water, cities, climate, oceans, and land. In other words, nature is absolutely crucial for giving us the basis on which we could mount actions through human measures that would ensure meeting the SDGs as specified. There are societal goals, including those for food, water, energy, health, and the achievement of human wellbeing for all, mitigating and adapting to climate change, and conserving and sustainably using nature. These can be achieved in sustainable pathways through the rapid and improved deployment of existing policy instruments and new initiatives that more effectively enlist individual and collective action for transformative change.

The key term that we need to consider here is the essential requirement of transformative change. If we are to meet some of the goals that would ensure sustainability over a period of time, then the change that would be required has to be transformative and urgent in every sense of the term. We must also bring in the Gandhian way of life because scientifically the IPBES has found that transformations towards sustainability are more likely when efforts are directed at the following key leverage points where efforts yield exceptionally large effects. These relate to : 1) visions of a good life; 2) total consumption; and waste; 3) values and action; 4) inequalities; 5) justice and inclusion in conservation; 6) externalities and telecouplings; 7) technology, innovation and investment, and 8) education and knowledge generation and sharing. Each one of these has a crucial role to play in ensuring that we bring about a rapid shift and transformative change which covers each of these aspects by which human society is convinced and motivated to implement measures that would ensure appropriate levels of transformation if we have to meet sustainability as laid down in the SDGs. In other words, a rapid and massive shift to the Gandhian view of life would give us a chance for a sustainable future.

It is also important to remember that feeding humanity and enhancing the conservation and sustainable use of nature are complementary and closely interdependent goals that can be advanced through sustainable agricultural, aqua cultural and livestock systems, the safeguarding of native species, varieties, breeds, and habitats, and ecological restoration. Nature essentially underpins the quality of life by providing basic life support for humanity as well as material goods and spiritual inspiration. Gandhi and his view of life embodies each one of these and, most importantly, it is built essentially on what we might interpret as spiritual inspiration. Nature's contributions in large measure are also important for human health and their decline, therefore would threaten a good quality of life. Today humanity is a dominant global influence on life on earth and has caused natural terrestrial, freshwater and marine ecosystems to decline. It is for this reason that the term anthropocene has been used to clearly indicate that the geological age that we are living in, even though far shorter than geological periods in the past, is essentially dominated by human activities as connoted by the term anthropocene. The global rate of species extinction is already at least 10 to 100s of times higher than the average rate over the past 10 million years and, unfortunately, it is accelerating. Overall, therefore, if we have to reduce the risks and minimize the decline from lifestyles and the quality of life, then it becomes absolutely essential that we bring about a major transformation in the current trends and practices because it is only on that basis that we can ensure a comprehensive reduction in all conditions that are currently contributing to, not only the growing risks from the impacts of climate change, but also in respect of a decline in ecosystem services which affect human society as a whole and all species on planet earth.

Hickel has put forward the view that growth can't possibly be green. He believes that green growth is a fallacy and he refers to the fact that many analysts and policymakers argue that all we need to do is to invest in more efficient technology and introduce the right incentives and we will then be able to keep growing while simultaneously reducing our impact on the natural world, which, according to him, is already at an unsustainable level. He shows this approach as one which probably aims at absolute decoupling of GDP from the total use of natural resources. He believes that while this may seem like an elegant solution, it otherwise is a catastrophic problem.

According to him, new evidence suggests that green growth is not the panacea everyone has been hoping for. In fact, it is not even possible. He then goes into looking at scenarios of the future where he believes that if, let us say, economic growth continued on its current trajectory, increasing at about two to three percent per year, then human consumption of natural resources, including fish, livestock, forests, metals, minerals, and fossil fuels would rise from 70 billion metric tons per year in 2012 to 180 billion metric tons per year by 2050. He believes that for a sustainable level of resource use, we would have to target about 50 billion metric tons per year, a boundary which was actually breached back in the year 2000.He then examines several scenarios for the future and assumes a tax that would raise the global price of carbon from \$50 to \$236 per metric ton and we could then assess the technological innovations that would double the efficiency with which we use resources. The analysis that he quotes actually leads to the global economy growing, let us say, by 3% per year, but that we would actually hit 95 billion metric tons of resource use by 2050. He, therefore, feels that merely providing a carbon tax is not going to result rapidly enough in a decoupling of the economy with respect to resource use. He even examines a scenario with carbon price which is a whopping \$573 per metric ton of tax slapped on a resource extraction tax and assumed rapid technological innovation spurred by strong government support.

All of this together, he feels, would still lead to 132 billion metric tons being reached by 2050. He believes that this outcome would be far worse than the other two previous studies because of what he terms as the rebound effect. This means that improvements in resource efficiency would drive down prices and cause demand to rise, thereby canceling out some of the gains. This is an issue which has been raised by researchers for quite some time because they feel that there could be a net effect in terms of increase in resource use simply because the price of alternatives might go down with imposition of a tax on the material or inputs that we are trying to target. As a result, we could have a substantial increase in demand, which clearly defeats the purpose. Hickel feels that by ending growth, we don't necessarily have to drive down living standards. He, in a sense, paraphrases what Gandhi said about the world having enough for everybody's need, but not for anybody's greed. Hickel feels that the planet provides more than enough for all of us. The problem is that resources are not equally distributed. He, therefore, altruistically believes that people's lives might be improved by sharing rather than plundering the resources of the earth.

George Monbiot, who is a distinguished columnist for The Guardian, and one who is capable of thinking deeply on issues that really define human society and the challenges that it faces, has written an interesting article with the title "While economic growth continues we'll never kick our fossil fuels habit". In a sense, he makes the same argument as Hickel because he says that for the first time in history, oil production is about to hit 100 million barrels per day. He also asks the question on how come the oil industry expects demand to climb until the 2030s. He believes that the answer lies in growth. There may be more electric vehicles on the world's roads, but there are also more internal combustion engines. This is a reality, which unfortunately is afflicting the developing countries far more than one finds the developed world really registered in recent years. The rate of growth in demand for automobiles, particularly SUVs, is at an all-time high in most parts of the developing world, whether it is China, India, Mexico or the countries of South East Asia.

Monbiot feels that what is particularly important is that with a growing economy, the money it generates stimulates high carbon industry. Anyone, who works in this field, knows environmental entrepreneurs, eco-consultants, and green business managers, who use their earnings to pay for holidays in distant parts of the world and flights required to get there. Electric vehicles have driven a new rush, particularly for lithium. As is now understood, the lithium ion battery is the main component of electric vehicles and, therefore, the demand for lithium will continue to go up as long as that particular battery is the mainstay of electric vehicles. Monbiot is particularly concerned about airport expansion because he believes that regardless of the availability and cost of flights, they are used disproportionately by the rich, as these are the people with their business meetings in New York, their second homes in Tuscany, and the money to pay for winter holidays, in the sun. Yet the impacts, which include noise, pollution of various kinds, and the effect in changing the climate are visited disproportionately on the poor. Monbiot sees a light at the end of the tunnel when he refers to Jacinda Ardern, the Prime Minister of New Zealand, who he has been quoted as mentioning "It will no longer be good enough to say a policy is successful because it increases GDP if it also degrades the physical environment."

The important issue is whether we are really prepared to change our measure of economic progress as relying exclusively on GDP to something that takes into account the impacts on the environment as such. As someone coming from the media, Monbiot also says that taken as a whole, the media is a threat to humanity. It claims to speak on our behalf, but it either speaks against us or does not speak at all. He, therefore, asks the question whether we should break the silence however uncomfortable it makes us and others feel. According to him, we should talk about the great unmentionables not just the breakdown in the climate system, but also growth and consumerism. He believes that we need to create a political space in which well-intentioned parties can act. He ends by saying let us bring a better world into being. This, to a large extent, accords with what Gandhi always believed in. We cannot possibly pattern our economic growth in different parts of the world on the basis of what has been achieved in the industrialized countries which essentially ushered in the Industrial Revolution. We, therefore, really need to look at the very basics of human development and the pattern by which we expand our economy. This would require almost a spiritual basis by which we reduce our demand, we cut down on materialism, and move away from what we have seen as the pattern in past growth of the economic system. At the same time, we must ensure that there is an increase in the efficiency of resource use in everything that we produce and everything that we consume and equity in the distribution of income and wealth.

All of this really means that we need to bring about a rapid shift to Gandhi. Half measures are really not going to work because we have a serious problem in terms of the major impacts that human activities are producing on the ecosystems of this earth, on the growing challenge of climate change the loss of biodiversity, and the degradation of ecosystems in most parts of the world. It is unfortunate that, those who pursue and practice neoclassical economics, some of whom are extremely distinguished and have even won the Nobel Prize in economic science, still continue to think within blinkers. The view that is often put forward is that if we were to, for instance, set our limits at warming of 1.5°C by the end of this century, then the cost to the economy would be so huge that the impoverishment that would take place as a result would make this a totally unacceptable limit to set. However, I think these economists need to be reminded of the fact that the inequitable impacts of climate change, of degradation of ecosystems, and the risks that climate change would pose to the most vulnerable sections of society would make human beings subject to dislocation and instability that, in every sense of the term, will afflict even the most prosperous regions of the globe.

At the cost of repetition, it needs to be kept in mind that the refugee problem, which has plagued Europe and parts of North America in recent years, will only get exacerbated with the impacts of climate change, with loss of biodiversity, with depletion of water resources, and all the basic wherewithal by which even the poorest of the poor must survive to keep their bodies and souls together. Unfortunately, neoclassical economists just do not consider the breakdown of some of these ecosystem services that are really of huge value to some of the poorest societies on earth. Consequently, for the assessment of neoclassical economists, which completely bypasses the damage and degradation to ecosystem services, provides a very shortsighted and myopic approach. We, therefore, need to make sure that policies to shift, for instance, to Gandhi's view of human existence are not dictated by dollars and cents because as long as these ignore and completely minimize the damage to ecosystems, the damage to the global commons and the serious risks associated with climate change, human society will be far worse off than if we were to moderate our demands and bring about a shift to what one might call a form of regrowth and not necessarily degrowth. More will be said about this in the following pages.

A very important article has recently been written by Stiglitz where he compares our current crisis to the equivalent of the Third World War. He asks a question whether at the stage of the Second World War, there was any person in the US who asked whether we could afford that war. It was clearly a case which reflected the existential threat of the Second World War, which would have engulfed every nation and every corner of this globe. He regards climate change as similar in its importance and the threat that it poses to what really happened during the Second World War. Stiglitz makes the argument that we can certainly afford dealing with the climate crisis with the right fiscal policies and a collective will. He also emphasizes the fact that most importantly we must afford it. He feels that our lives and civilization, as we know it, are at stake just as they were in the Second World War. He says we are already experiencing the direct costs of ignoring this issue because in recent years, the country has lost almost 2% of GDP in weather related disasters, which include floods, hurricanes, and forest fires. The cost to our health from climate related diseases is just being tabulated, but he feels that too will run into the tens of billions of dollars. Of course, there is no mention of the uncounted number of lives lost. He believes we will pay for the climate breakdown one way or the other so it makes sense to spend money now to reduce emissions rather than wait until later to pay a lot more for the consequences. Among these, of course, would be the major impacts and risks associated with sea level rise.

It is refreshing to see that Stiglitz, an economist who has always been ahead of his time, is really taking an appropriate view of what climate change means to human society and to all the ecosystems on planet Earth. He also believes that if the climate emergency and the war on it is to be carried out in an appropriate manner, then it would be good for the economy, just as the Second World War set the stage for America's golden economic era, with the fastest rate of growth in its history amidst shared prosperity. He believes that the Green New Deal, which is now being discussed in Congress, would stimulate demand ensuring that all available resources were used and the transition to the green economy would likely usher in a new boom. He believes that Trump's focus on the industries of the past like coal, is strangling the much more sensible move to wind and solar power. Stiglitz believes that far more jobs will be created in renewable energy than we would lose in coal.

Stiglitz's views, as put forward in this article, are indeed refreshing because they give substance to the thesis conveyed in these pages that we really do not mean degrowth, what we need is regrowth. This, of course, becomes totally relevant for a country like India and many other developing countries because most of the population is still living in rural areas. However, the developing countries have more or less followed the path of the developed world by setting up large cities and areas which contain several millions of their population, which naturally provide jobs and employment opportunities, simply because most of the resources of these countries go into urban development. That generates industrial activities in these areas and provision of the infrastructure that generates employment for those who are migrating into these urban centers from rural areas.

It appears that perhaps the regrowth that one is proposing in the thesis conveyed in these pages embracing the original philosophy of Gandhi, is an issue that needs deliberate and careful reflection. Just as in the period of the Industrial Revolution in the developed countries, urbanization was the basic plank on which industrialization took place. What we need to consider now is an approach that essentially reduces urbanization as an attractive form of economic activities, but essentially diffuses the urban population and moves it away to rural areas. As it happens, with technologies that are available today including access to the internet and development of public transport going into rural areas, it is entirely possible that we take a regional approach which contains plans and strategies both for urban as well as complementary rural development. This will provide jobs, not only in urban areas, but also in rural locations. Hence, we need now to look not merely at urban centers and what they represent in terms of investment opportunities and growth of infrastructure and employment, but take a far more integrated view by which an entire rural hinterland that serves and works with urban locations can be considered as a unit for attracting investments, for generating employment, and for ensuring that there is a healthy quality of life that keeps rural populations anchored down in their original locations, rather than large numbers of people moving into slums in the cities involving an absolutely miserable state of living and a deteriorating quality of life.

It would, therefore, be useful to look at how demographic trends are moving even in the developed world. To some extent, the trends that we see beginning now are in some sense a justification of what Gandhi said about Western civilization wondering whether in the future they would ask "What have we done?"

****

Anticipating impacts of climate change

by

Dr. Ash Pachauri

A call for action to achieve safe and sustainable self-care waste management

Although the practice of self-care can be traced back to the ages when communities traditionally cared for themselves by using varieties of medicines prepared from natural herbs, roots, and plants as well as animal parts, the concept of self-care itself was officially only recognized by the World Health Organization (WHO) in the 1980s. WHO defines self-care as "the activities individuals, families, and communities undertake with the intention of enhancing health, preventing disease, limiting illness, and restoring health. These activities are derived from knowledge and skills from the pool of both professional and lay experience. In 2016, WHO adopted the Framework on Integrated, People-Centered Health Services defining self-care as "putting people and communities, not diseases, at the centers of health systems and empowering people to take charge of their own health rather than being passive recipients of services" (1). Literature clearly suggests that self-care will continue to grow in importance especially as it is seen as a key approach to reach Universal Health Coverage (UHC) (2) (3).

Acknowledging the growing role and importance of self-care interventions, WHO recently developed and launched normative guidelines on self-care (4). This was done with a vision to support countries with evidence-based, person-centered guidance across the life-course on self-care interventions for health. These guidelines must be adapted to meet the unique needs of different populations in various social, economic, and cultural contexts. Given WHO's vision for self-care in achieving UHC, which is recognized as a unifying platform for making progress on the Sustainable Development Goal (SDG) 3 for health, it is imperative that the self-care system itself be made sustainable as it addresses future needs (5). As we reduce dependence on hospital-based systems and enhance our reliance on person-cantered ones, supported by technology, and as more services are adopted exclusively by the layperson in communities and homes, we will need a multisectoral approach that looks at all facets of the self-care system (6). For the self-care system to be sustainable, it will need to address changing patterns of self-care consumption, develop more efficient production methods, and adopt safe waste management techniques while also preventing waste. Currently, improper health care waste management practices put over half the world's population at risk from occupational, environmental, and public health threats (7). What adds a sense of urgency to the issue is the implications of growing self-care product waste which is manifold and has been largely overlooked until now. Furthermore, unlike waste generated within healthcare facilities, management of self-care products' waste still remains unregulated.

A famous, ancient Zen proverb says *"It takes a wise man to learn from his mistakes, but an even wiser man to learn from other's mistakes."* We must learn from past experience and the valuable lessons offered by other fields. The clean energy promise of solar panels made over 40 years ago advocated for "clean" solar technology. At that stage, we did not consider its end-of-life stage management. Today, unsafe waste management of solar technology itself puts us at risk of environmental and health disasters, especially in the poorest countries – including, Ghana, Nigeria, Vietnam, India, Pakistan, and Bangladesh – which are dumped with much of the solar waste made up of carcinogenic cadmium, lead, and other toxins (8). This is just one example, among many, of our failure to consider the end-of-life or disposal of products when promoting them with all good intentions to protect the wellbeing of communities, and especially, the most vulnerable.

In the words of Gandhi *"As human beings our greatness lies not so much in being able to remake the world...as in being able to remake ourselves"*. With just over a decade available before the world evaluates its success in attaining UHC and the SDGs, there is a critical need to create sustainable responses for better health, especially for the most vulnerable and marginalized communities. The costs of inaction threaten the existence of our planet and the health of future generations.

This is an urgent call for mindful action by multiple players working at different levels to understand the sustainability implications of waste management and to play individual and interdependent roles in facilitating the development of programs to promote safe and sustainable self-care waste management.

References

1. WHO | What are integrated people-centred health services?

2. Service WHOHE. Health education in self-care: possibilities and limitations. 1984

3. Levin LS, Idler EL. Self-Care in Health. Annu Rev Public Health. 1983;4(1):181–201.

4. WHO | WHO consolidated guideline on self-care interventions for health: sexual and reproductive health and rights.

5. WHO | WHO core principles for achieving safe and sustainable manage-

ment of health-care waste: Policy paper.

6. Pachauri A, Shah P, Almroth BC, Sevilla NPM, Narasimhan M. Safe and sustainable waste management of self care products. BMJ. 2019 Apr 1;365:l1298.

7. Harhay MO, Halpern SD, Harhay JS, Olliaro PL. Health care waste management: a neglected and growing public health problem worldwide. Trop Med Int Health. 2009 Nov 1;14(11):1414–7.

8. Shellenberger, M. If Solar Panels Are So Clean, Why Do They Produce So Much Toxic Waste? Forbes 2018, May 23. Retrieved from https://www.forbes.com/sites/michaelshellenberger/2018/05/23/if-solar-panels-are-so-clean-why-do-they-produce-so-much-toxic-waste/#35bfd4fa121c on October 17, 2019.

When We Become Village Minded

It is entirely true that even in the developed countries, rural areas have largely been neglected, and in the case of the US, for instance, a large number of farms, particularly the ones that have huge areas of acreage, are owned by agribusinesses. So the result is that while all these farms have been mechanized, they have used technologies that essentially displace labor. The result is that very few jobs have been generated in rural areas, and, therefore, there is an ongoing migration of people moving from rural into urban locations. The European Council on Foreign Relations has interestingly brought out a commentary by Caroline de Gruyter which has the title of "The revenge of the countryside". It starts with a plea that Europe must narrow the gap between urban and rural areas, otherwise, radical populists will continue to flourish in neglected communities. The author refers to the Brexit vote which the British people seem to have favored in a manner that has led to a serious political crisis in that country. She refers to the fact that people voted to get out of the European Union (EU) for many reasons. But it is hard to avoid the sense that the result was in part driven by a desire to deal a blow to the UK's urban, cosmopolitan elite. She takes the view that this elite has obviously profited from globalization, while prospects for rural communities have remained stagnant.

In some sense, the international trading system also orients itself to providing prosperity to urban dwellers, often enriching those who are already prosperous and completely neglecting those rural populations which really have no wealth or income levels which would ensure their full participation in international trade. The author also refers to the problem in Belgium where the region of Wallonia is poor and feels neglected. It was in the 19th century that Wallonia's steel and coal mining industries prospered. But the result has been that the mines were closed after the Second World War, and the region, therefore, has been moving downhill as a result. Consequently, unemployment is high and generations of families are living on government doles. The gap between urban and rural communities is widening all over Europe, increasingly causing political fallouts at the continental level, according to the author. As a result, it divides Europeans, allows vulnerable electorates to be seduced by populists, and makes it harder for the EU to formulate common trade and foreign policies. In Austria, for instance, there is a direct link between depopulation and the relative neglect of the countryside. Overall, the picture that the author provides is one of rural areas being neglected for decades. As a result of which, the inequitable distribution of wealth and opportunities for growth, have only become exacerbated overtime.

In the case of the US, a paper by Brookings published in 2018, refers to the fact that recently released census data for the first seven years of the decade indicate a resumption of the population dispersal that was put on hold for a good part of the post Great Recession period. The estimates indicate a revival of suburbanization and movement to rural areas along with Snowbelt to Sun Belt population shifts. The paper also refers to the fact that the data show new dispersal to large and moderate size metro areas in the middle of the country, especially in the Northeast and Midwest. It concludes that if these shifts continue, they could call into question the sharp clustering of the nation's population in large metropolitan areas and cities, which clearly characterized the first half of the 2010s. The paper also refers to the fact that suburbanization is on the rise, even though in the wake of the 2008 recession that affected all parts of the globe, this trend was on hold. However, the trends through 2016 and 2017, as shown in the figure below, seem to indicate some changes in these trends.

Figure 4

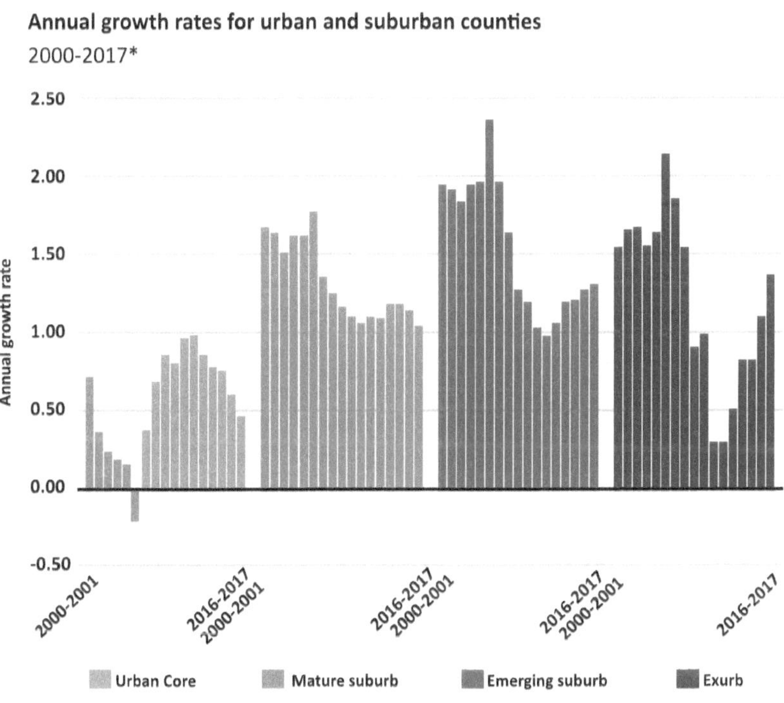

The paper also refers to revived suburban and exurban growth seems to be most pronounced in the Sun Belt metropolitan areas. While these suburbanization trends have not yet reached the levels of the early 2000s, they do seem to be associated with recent improvements in the economy and the housing market that have clearly removed the constraints to suburban relocation among potential movers, including, in particular, young adult millennial households. For this reason, the paper concludes that there is reason to believe the trend is likely to continue. There is also a clear indication that a shift to smaller metropolitan areas and counties outside metropolitan areas is in evidence. This is brought out by the figure provided below.

Figure 5

Annual growth rates for metropolitan and non-metropolitan areas
2000-2017

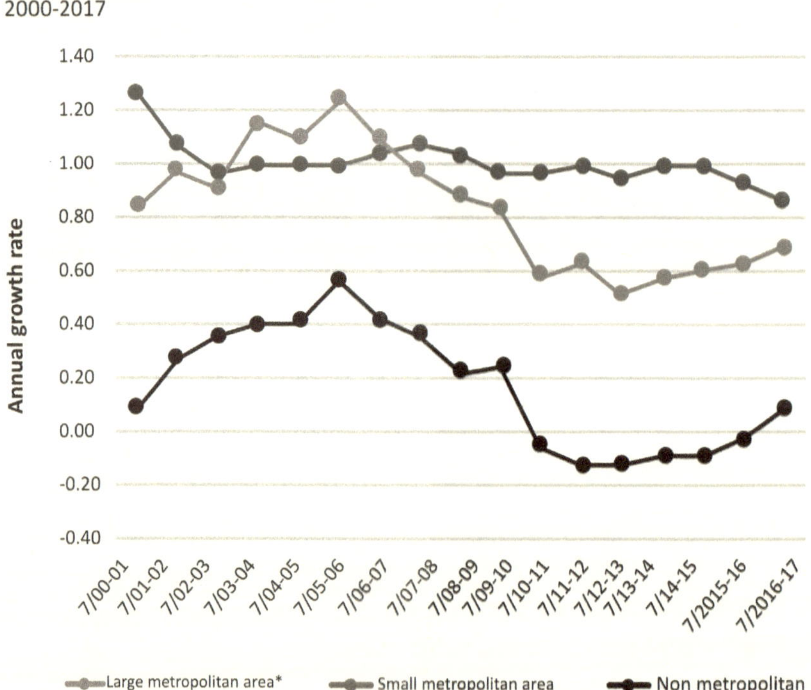

*Large metropolitan area have populations greater than 500,000

There is no doubt that large metropolitan areas continue to grow much faster than the rest of the country. But it appears that the trends are moving in the direction which remind us of the early 2000s when small metropolitan growth exceeded that in large areas and non-metropolitan growth was much higher than it is now. The shift towards smaller areas is evident from domestic migration statistics, according to the paper.

A document from the Pew Research Center has also looked at trends in recent years which have reshaped the overall US population in terms of racial and ethnic diversity, increasing immigration, and rising number of older adults. It concludes that recent US population growth has been uneven. Urban counties have grown at roughly the overall national rate of 13% since the year 2000 and suburban and small metropolitan areas have grown more briskly. Rural counties, according to this paper, have lagged and half of them have fewer residents now than they did in the year 2000. In some sense, therefore, the US situation parallels that in Europe because obviously rural locations do not, in any way, attract population movements on account of lower employment opportunities, less than satisfactory infrastructure facilities, and a whole range of other conditions which define the quality of life. What is particularly relevant is to look at the opportunities that rural areas provide in view of the trend in terms of growth of urban populations and if we were to evaluate regrowth opportunities, clearly there would be, as Stiglitz has pointed out, no reason why growth itself would stop. But what we would get as a result would be growth that is far more desirable and certainly far more supportive of a much higher quality of life.

To some extent, therefore, we would have a large number of stranded assets in urban areas in the developed world, and, therefore, the trend towards moving populations creating employment opportunities and investments in infrastructure would be a part of the regrowth effort in rural areas. This may turn out to be slower than what we would find in the developing countries.

It is true that the developing countries, which are still in the process of establishing a pattern of growth, which defines the future would find it far more effective, and in some sense, far more facile, to be able to create rural employment and economic opportunities. In some sense this would be much easier than would be the case in the developed world.

It should also be kept in mind that to bring about this pattern of development would involve a much stronger effort at integrated development wherein urban areas would need to be considered as a complementary whole for rural locations that are clearly tied in with urban areas which are possibly today the main centers of economic development and employment opportunities. One example of an integrated approach has been discussed earlier in these pages, but this clearly means that while municipalities and local government in urban locations would be extremely important in laying out a strategy for the future, coordination among municipalities as well as local government in rural areas would be an important part of such an integrated approach. This necessarily means that institutional mechanisms will have to be found by which an integrated approach is followed. Unfortunately in the past, these institutions have not really evolved and have, therefore, been ineffective in defining opportunities which are consistent with this type of approach.

It would really require proper coordination mechanisms by which we can take an integrated and area-oriented approach involving urban as well as rural locations and this, to a large extent, would also be very helpful for urban locations, because it is entirely true that a number of urban locations these days find it very difficult to keep up with the demand for infrastructure, to keep up with water supply, electricity, sanitation and other facilities including environmental benefits. Consequently, an area approach which also ensures that there is depopulation from urban to rural locations would actually even help in the governance of urban locations which would, for some time, remain at the center of the integrated approach which is being advocated.

It is clear that a radical change, which is needed at this stage, cannot be brought about unless there is a disruptive approach to the status quo. There is far too much bureaucratic and political inertia, which is likely to bring about resistance to change that would really help the world move towards a sustainable pattern of development and enhanced human happiness based on Gandhian values. It is also an established fact that policies and programs, which current institutions pursue, are generally meant to protect the interests of those who are part of the system. It was in the early 1980s that Mrs. Indira Gandhi, when she was Prime Minister of India, did not allow the Silent Valley hydro-electric project in the state of *Kerala* because it would have endangered, and possibly rendered extinct, a particular species of primate as well as other forms of biodiversity. This author was the Chair of a committee which was asked to look at alternative sites which could allow a power project somewhat similar to Silent Valley. During the course of inspection of these alternative sites, when a large number of the officials of the power utility were present, one of them remarked at the end of the visit "Sir, please recommend at least one site because otherwise we will all retire as executive engineers". Bureaucracies have been converted into silos and managers and officials essentially become self-seeking individuals who naturally keep their career interests as paramount.

There are also vested interests that seldom allow change, simply because it may go against their own narrow and short term interests. There are news reports that the fossil fuel lobby has spent about one billion dollars to resist any action to mitigate emissions of carbon dioxide, and thereby delay research and development and commercialization of substitutes such as renewable energy technologies.

A disruptive and short time-bound approach could carry the benefit of a rapidly moving target, which may perhaps not allow the galvanization of resistance and a coalition of vested interests who would try to thwart action.

Hence, a major shift to Gandhi's values and priorities would be far more effective than incremental measures which may die out before they ever reach culmination.

Healthy Discontent is Prelude to Progress

The question arises on what does all this add up to. We are obviously at a stage where the disastrous trends around us need to be halted, since their dire consequences would probably be seen in a short period of time. A solution to this would only work if as McDuff states we need to throw the kitchen sink at this because he believes that policy tweaks like carbon tax will really not do. He also stated that the impact of a dramatic reconfiguration of the industrial economy requires similarly large changes in the welfare state. In some sense, this view accords with Mahatma Gandhi's own interpretation of what is wrong with human society at this point of time. Gandhi's clear interpretation of the fact that non-violence is the only solution for some of the ills in this society included a clear understanding that the manifestation of violent behavior is seen every day in the exploitation of one group of individuals by another.

It is truly tragic that even when it comes to waging wars between one country and another there is hardly any sense of remorse even when these wars lead to prolonged and untold suffering. A case in point is the manner in which the US conducted its war in Afghanistan against Soviet occupation, for which they harnessed terrorist organizations and created a major terrorist force called the Taliban. If we look at the war in Iraq, it was clearly manufactured on the basis of lies and falsehoods, wherein the US at the highest level stated that we need to mount that war because Iraq possessed weapons of mass destruction. Over time it became clear that this falsehood had no bearing on the truth, because Iraq certainly did not have any weapons of mass destruction. The result of that war and the enormous disruption it caused to Iraqi society is what resulted in the Islamic state (ISIS), which has resulted in atrocities of the worst kind in various parts of the world.

Basically what we need is a major shift to the Gandhian way of thinking and if one could describe such a shift it would have to be tectonic in nature. In other words, we have to throw the kitchen sink at the current system and make sure that we bring about a substantial amount of change in our thinking, our values, and the very concept of economic growth and development. Gandhi's belief was conveyed in his words.

"My religion is based on truth and non-violence. Truth is my God. Non-violence is the greatest means of realizing Him. It is the greatest force at the disposal of mankind. It is mightier than the mightiest weapon of destruction devised by the ingenuity of man." He also said "In one who has *ahimsa* (non-violence) in him becomes part of his very nature. Perfect non-violence is the highest bravery. Non-violent conduct is never demoralizing, cowardice always is."

If we have to bring about a major shift in the values and beliefs of human society then clearly this is something which cannot be spread over a period of time because if that were to be, we would be faced with inevitable disaster and catastrophe, which would overtake every part of human society and certainly this planet which is our only home. There is, therefore, the imperative of bringing about a major shift in the manner in which we view happiness, the manner in which we seek personal satisfaction, and the need for laying down certain guardrails beyond which we do not venture over a period of time so that the acts of violence that we see all around us do not remain a part of human behavior. Ever since the advent of industrialization we have seen the inexorable march of events and human desires which has led us to a stage where all forms and means of economic development and growth are centered around a single model. Gandhi's emphasis on governance at the lowest level where he has talked about Panchayats, which in India are the grassroots level organizations in villages, was clearly designed to move away from this single model of development or a mono-culture of urbanization and nuclear families. These are clearly ill suited to the practice of non-violence and oriented essentially towards material wants and their satisfaction combined with the trend of urbanization. These have been brought in by the industrialized countries of the West with the consequence of growing disparities in income and wealth which clearly are a source of major social disruption and instability in several parts of the world. In 2019 there has been a spate of demonstrations and protests in countries spread across from Chile to Lebanon and to France, wherein those who are at the bottom rung of the ladder are clearly very resentful of the fact that a very small and privileged group of people own the assets and wealth equivalent to those of the large majority of the poor.

In this respect the Oxfam reports are relevant, because they have progressively shown how a small number of people seems to be commanding income and wealth over a growing number of the poor across the world. This is something that Gandhi clearly saw as a form of violence of one group versus the other. Similarly he saw capital not as something that we could do away with, but the evil that is associated with the inequitable use of capital and its total lack of sensitivity towards the welfare of the people, needs to be removed. In the model that Gandhi advocated as being in the interests of human society owners of capital should regard themselves as trustees on behalf of the people.

We are also living in a world where there is a massive loss of biodiversity, damage to the earth's ecosystems, and most significantly the problem of human induced climate change. All of these will certainly make it very difficult for today's younger generation and those coming after them to be able to live with a sense of security.

The risks associated with climate change are going to mount progressively over time and in a disproportionate manner, which would make it extremely hazardous for human society to live in several areas, many of which are very vulnerable and unfortunately happen to be in some of the poorest countries of the world. To deal with climate change would require a major shift towards Gandhian philosophy because unless one brings about a major change in the way we see and visualize growth and development, we are not likely to be able to, as mentioned earlier, tweak the current system and bring about solutions to the problem of growing impacts of climate change. In this regard the time has come for human beings to not regard GDP growth as the gospel and ensure that we come up with a set of indicators which accurately reflect the welfare of human society and do not at any stage give us the false belief that mere growth of GDP is the be-all and end-all of human existence. For this purpose we would need to make sure that, for instance, subsidies which have a distortionary impact on our welfare, are removed as rapidly as possible. In 2019, the International Monetary Fund (IMF) estimated the subsidies on fossil fuels are clearly staggering in nature.

We necessarily, therefore, have to create institutions which ensure a certain level of equity and fairness but do not in any way allow us to prolong the systems by which we have been measuring economic growth and development in the past. Gandhi's tributes to nature and his worship of nature are totally appropriate in terms of every human being being able to get access to the beauty of nature. This clearly is at enormous variance from the lure of material goods and services which we have been hankering after since the beginning of industrialization, and more particularly since the end of the Second World War.

The challenge really is on how we might be able to bring about this tectonic shift to the Gandhian way of thinking. Firstly we have on this planet more than seven billion people whose collective desires and preferences point essentially in the direction of what has already been established by the industrialized countries. Their values, their aspirations, and their desires are essentially dictated by what has taken place over a century and a half of evolution of human values and what underlies human activity. Over and above that, we have the enormous power of vested interests, essentially symbolized by the massive amount of advertising expenditure that takes place globally, and which has been rising since several decades.

The economic system that essentially incorporates the extent of advertising, the promotion of new goods and services which are seen to constitute the paths to human happiness, clearly needs to be changed and we would have to throw the kitchen sink at this also. How do we bring about this kind of shift? Gandhi would have celebrated his 150th anniversary on the 2nd of October 2019. This is a fitting moment for us to reflect on the wisdom and truth that this human being was able to preach on the basis of what he always practiced. What is needed today is perhaps an understanding by the leaders of various faiths on why we need to shift gears and change direction. It is heartening that Pope Francis has been ahead of most leaders of faith and has candidly expressed his views advocating a much simpler form of living, a deeper respect for nature, and the need for us to care for the creation around us. However, this message needs to be spread to other faiths in the world. We also need, at least a group of world leaders, who are prepared to swim against the tide and to show us that if we do not accept the Gandhian view and bring it into our lives as rapidly as possible, then we would have untold misery and perhaps a catastrophe far beyond our expectations in a short period of time.

We have a number of nuclear weapons in different countries of the world and as yet there is no attempt at all at the global level to do away with these massive sources of destruction and also other weapons which are used in conventional forms of warfare. Can we possibly spread the word and ensure that Gandhi's message does not remain confined to what he was able to do in his lifetime but goes far beyond because it is relevant today perhaps far more than it was during his life. There are of course politicians and leaders on the extreme left and on the extreme right who are currently putting forward their credentials as being able to solve the world's problems. Often the views that they represent are backward in nature and extremely limiting in what they represent.

The huge right wing response to migration, which is bound to increase particularly with disparities in income and the impacts of climate change, is an aberration which needs to be nipped in the bud as quickly as possible. There is, of course, a great deal of concern about capitalism. It may be useful to recall the quotation provided in the earlier pages of this work "ending climate change requires the end of capitalism. Have we got the stomach for it?" Capitalism as it is practiced obviously has a growing number of distortions which have to be done away with. But to suggest solutions that lie in extreme forms of crony capitalism, socialism, or communism would clearly be extremely harmful to human society.

For a start, I think we need to revisit the whole pattern of urbanized growth which clearly is responsible for a large number of the ills that we see before us today. For instance, when it comes to emissions of greenhouse gasses resulting in human induced climate change, around two thirds of the total global emissions emanate from urban areas. Over and above that, we know that the problem of disparities in income and wealth is essentially a part of the urban phenomenon. This is not to say that rural areas are in any way more virtuous and that we would not have disparities of income and wealth over there. After all, throughout the ages, there have been landlords who have used labor almost as would be the case with slave labor. But in this day and age, where we have essentially democratic systems of government and regulations, which clearly lay down some requirements for ownership of land, the manner in which labor is employed, and the various regulations which protect labor from several forms of exploitation, can be effective. Gandhi's view of bringing about development in rural areas is perhaps something that might be the most prudent action to take if we want to bring about a tectonic shift and a transformation of current society.

This approach also answers some of the doubts which are being expressed openly and widely about the continuation of economic growth in the manner that we have seen over the past several decades. Essentially, we are now aware that the era of high economic growth, as was the case in several industrial nations, is now over. Therefore, rather than embark on a phase of degrowth, which many ecological economists and others are advocating, what we need is a process of regrowth, by which those very regions, those rural areas and communities which have been deprived in the past, require a major shift in policies by which we bring about regrowth focused in these areas. This would, not only ensure that we achieve a far more equitable and balanced process of growth, but also a period when we harness human as well as technological resources to meet some of the challenges of those regions which have been neglected for many decades in the past. It is also essential to put in place regulatory and legislative measures by which we create institutions at the grassroots level, which are empowered, which develop the capacity and human capital by which they can take decisions on their own rather than rely on the layers above them. A top-down approach would clearly not be in touch with the will and the wants of the people. We, therefore, need to bring about this period of regrowth and a shift in priorities that do not in any way continue with the huge subsidies, for instance, which the fossil fuels industry has been receiving for much too long, or for that matter, the kind of advertising expenditure that the tobacco industry is able to command. Some very clearcut policies, regulatory measures, and legislative steps would require to be taken to ensure that we bring about this shift towards deprived and rural locations which would ensure regrowth rather than a period of regrowth.

Since Gandhi was the Father of the Nation for all Indians, any initiative to bring about transformative change would rightly need to originate in India. However, since we are dealing with a global challenge, it is absolutely essential that a core group of countries should be part of any initiative that involves a radical shift from the current pattern of development to what has a large Gandhian content. To this end perhaps India has to convince, to begin with, the BRICS countries (Brazil, Russia, India, China, and South Africa). To this one could add a large country like Indonesia and an important country of Latin America like Mexico. The BRICS grouping could therefore be extended to IMBRICS which includes Indonesia and Mexico. It was in 1947 that Gandhi and the Government of India, even before Independence, organized the Asian Relations Conference. It would be most fitting and important to arrive at a culmination of efforts ending in 2022 to celebrate 75 years since the Asian Relations Conference. The actions that need to be taken on a coordinated multi-country basis should be as follows:

1. We need to get rid of the measure of GDP as a commonly accepted value to measure human progress. This is something that the Secretary General of the United Nations must treat as his mission. He should set up a group that not only comes up with an accurate measure of human wellbeing and wellness but actually make efforts to sell this concept to all the countries in the world. Here again, India has to find a way by which it convinces the UN Secretary General of the value of such an initiative.

2. What is needed immediately is a price on carbon. Even though with the resistance that exists in several parts of the world, particularly among many oil exporting countries, this would be a very difficult outcome to

arrange. But with all the attention that is now being provided on the seriousness of climate change, perhaps a Conference of the Parties under the UNFCCC would be the best place to initiate a price on carbon which is uniform across the developed world, but which takes into account the "Common but Differentiated Responsibility" across different countries. The grouping of IMBRICS could be sensitized on this issue even though Russia, as an oil exporter, may be reluctant to join in. However, this may not be a difficult task if all the other countries are willing to go ahead on this issue and effect the adoption of a price on carbon.

3. There is a need for a Youth Summit which should be held in 2021. This summit need not take place in one location, but should be held in different parts of the world, ensuring that young people do not merely protest or demonstrate but actually take action within their own spheres of activity and influence. A detailed blueprint for such an action can be prepared, possibly as part of the POP (Protect Our Planet) Movement. If we look at just the universities across the world, the estimate of the POP Movement is that over 2 gigatonnes of $CO2$ are emitted annually by universities and colleges across the world. If the youth in the universities and the faculty get involved, it should be possible to cut down on these emissions by 20% within a period of three years.

4. It would be important to mobilize leaders of different faiths to focus on climate change. Inherently every scripture in every religion highlights the need for protecting nature and respecting the divine work of our Creator. Perhaps, such a summit of faith leaders, could be held in the land of Buddha, in India where Pope Francis could be invited as a convenor, along with leaders of Islam, Hinduism, Buddhism, Sikhism, Jainism, Judaism, and other faiths. It would have been most convenient to convene such a summit at the Vatican but it is possible that some leaders may not be willing to go to the Vatican for an event of this nature. Hence, a neutral location, which has no semblance of a religious presence, would be most appropriate given the fact that the land of Buddha hardly has any followers of Buddhism. A summit of faith leaders could be convened there without any reluctance on the part of those

who are to be invited.

It was just recently that President Gorbachev expressed the view that as long as weapons of destruction existed in the world, we would be living in dangerous times. The 75th anniversary of the Asian Relations Conference in 2022 would be an occasion when leaders of the world commit themselves to reducing their weapons and ushering in a period of peace. After all, Gandhi equated violence with the expression of greed and avarice, which results in the multiplication of our material demands. Hence if violence is reduced and done away with, it should be possible for us to respect nature, even resuscitate the wealth of nature and focus on values that are at the heart of human happiness.

In all this effort an understanding between India and China would be crucially important, not only because these are the most populous nations on earth but also because China and India represent ancient civilizations which have survived over several centuries. Besides, given the power of China's economic growth and its position as the second largest economy in the world, makes it essential that it is a participant in moving to Gandhi. In any case Gandhi's philosophy is spread similar to that of the sages in China going back to Confucius and Lao Tzu.

What is being proposed is certainly not a simple task, but if we look at the alternative which involves "do nothing"; then the choice becomes very clear. Gandhi rightly said "A violent and bloody revolution is a certainty one day unless there is a voluntary abdication of riches and power that riches give and sharing them for the common good."

Indeed, we are already seeing signs of revolt in different societies and communities and these would only increase as the complexity of our predicament becomes much worse over time. The time to act, therefore, is now. If we postpone action to a later date and if we remain oblivious to the catastrophe that we would be facing in the future and our children and their children would suffer the consequences that are difficult to comprehend at the stage.

The 150th birth anniversary of Gandhi reminds us of the direction in which we need to travel, and travel instantly.

Select References

Dandabathula G, Bhardwaj P, Burra M, Rao PVVP, Rao SS. Impact assessment of India's Swachh Bharat Mission - Clean India Campaign on acute diarrheal disease outbreaks: Yes, there is a positive change. J Fam Med Prim Care. 2019 Mar;8(3):1202–8.

Galbraith, John Kenneth, 1908-2006. The Affluent Society. Boston: Houghton Mifflin, 1976.

Global Network on Energy for Sustainable Development (GNESD) – UNEP-CCC. (2019, May 15). UNEP-CCC. https://unepccc.org/project/global-network-on-energy-for-sustainable-development-gnesd/

Greater Good. How nature can make you kinder, happier, and more creative. (n.d.). Greater Good. https://greatergood.berkeley.edu/article/item/how_nature_makes_you_kinder_happier_more_creative

Groh, S. P. &. S. P. &. S. (2018). A critical review of modern approaches for multidimensional energy poverty measurement. *ideas.repec.org*. https://ideas.repec.org/a/bla/wireae/v7y2018i6ne304.html

Harhay MO, Halpern SD, Harhay JS, Olliaro PL. Health care waste management: a neglected and growing public health problem worldwide. Trop Med Int Health. 2009 Nov 1;14(11):1414–7.

Hickel, Jason (2019) "Degrowth: a theory of radical abundance", real-world economics review, issue no. 87, 19. March, pp 54-68.

International Labor Organization (ILO) Global Employment Trends 2014 – Risk of a jobless recovery? (ilo.org).

International Monetary Fund (IMF) Shang, D. C. W. P. L. (2019, May 2). *Global fossil fuel subsidies remain large: an update based on Country-Level estimates.* IMF. https://www.imf.org/en/Publications/WP/Issues/2019/05/02/Global-Fossil-Fuel-Subsidies-Remain-Large-An-Update-Based-on-Country-Level-Estimates-46509

Intergovernmental Panel on Climate Change (IPCC) Fourth Assessment Report (AR4) https://www.ipcc.ch/assessment-report/ar4/

Intergovernmental Panel on Climate Change (IPCC) Fifth Assessment Report (AR5) https://www.ipcc.ch/assessment-report/ar5/

Intergovernmental Panel on Climate Change (IPCC) Special Report on Climate Change and Land — IPCC site. (n.d.). Special Report on Climate Change and Land. https://www.ipcc.ch/srccl/

Intergovernmental Panel on Climate Change (IPCC) Special report on the Ocean and cryosphere in a changing climate —. (n.d.). Special Report on the Ocean and Cryosphere in a Changing Climate. https://www.ipcc.ch/srocc/

Intergovernmental Panel on Climate Change (IPCC) Summary for policy-makers — Global warming of 1.5 OC. (n.d.). Global Warming of 1.5 °C. https://www.ipcc.ch/sr15/chapter/spm/

IPBES Report 2019 Global Assessment Report on Biodiversity and Ecosystem Services https://www.ipbes.net/global-assessment

Keynes, J. M. (1930). Economic possibilities for our grandchildren. In Essays in Persuasion

Levin LS, Idler EL. Self-Care in Health. Annu Rev Public Health. 1983;4(1):181–201.

McDuff, P. (2020, February 3). It's fashionable to be 'politically homeless'. But it's also callous and detached. *The Guardian*. https://www.theguardian.com/commentisfree/2019/dec/05/politically-homeless-austerity-election

MK Gandhi https://www.mkgandhi.org/articles/g_edu.htm

Monbiot, G. (2021, August 25). While economic growth continues we'll never kick our fossil fuels habit. *The Guardian*. https://www.theguardian.com/commentisfree/2018/sep/26/economic-growth-fossil-fuels-habit-oil-industry?CMP=share_btn_tw

Nuccitelli, D. (2021, August 25). Scientists warned the US president about global warming 50 years ago today. The Guardian. https://www.theguardian.com/environment/climate-consensus-97-per-cent/2015/nov/05/scientists-warned-the-president-about-global-warming-50-years-ago-today

Oxfam, *Annual Report 2019*. (2019, November 14). Oxfam. https://www.oxfamamerica.org/explore/research-publications/annual-report-2019/

Pachauri, S. (2011). Reaching an international consensus on defining modern energy access. *Current Opinion in Environmental Sustainability*, 3(4), 235–240. https://doi.org/10.1016/j.cosust.2011.07.005

Pachauri, S., & Spreng, D. (2011). Measuring and monitoring energy poverty. *Energy Policy*, 39(12), 7497–7504. https://doi.org/10.1016/j.enpol.2011.07.008

Pachauri A, Shah P, Almroth BC, Sevilla NPM, Narasimhan M. Safe and sustainable waste management of self care products. BMJ. 2019 Apr 1;365:l1298.

Pew Research Center https://www.pewresearch.org/

Practical Action. (2021, June 13). *Poor People's Energy Outlook 2012 - Practical Action.* https://practicalaction.org/knowledge-centre/resources/poor-peoples-energy-outlook-2012/

Project MUSE - Brookings Papers on Economic Activity-Fall 2018. (n.d.). https://muse.jhu.edu/issue/40841

POP Movement: www.thepopmovement.org

Richards, J. (2016, January 18). *George Bernard Shaw Poem, "We are the living graves of murdered beasts"* Humane Decisions. https://humanedecisions.com/george-bernard-shaw-poem-we-are-the-living-graves-of-murdered-beasts/

RK Pachauri www.rkpachauri.org

Report of the Education Commission (1964-66): Education and National Development https://archive.org/stream/ReportOfTheEducationCommission1964-66D.S.KothariReport/48.Jp-ReportOfTheEducationCommission1964-66d.s.kothari_djvu.txt

Service WHOHE. Health education in self-care: possibilities and limitations. 1984

Shellenberger, M. If Solar Panels Are So Clean, Why Do They Produce So Much Toxic Waste? Forbes 2018, May 23. Retrieved from https://www.forbes.com/sites/michaelshellenberger/2018/05/23/if-solar-panels-are

-so-clean-why-do-they-produce-so-much-toxic-waste/#35bfd4fa121con
October 17, 2019.

Stanford researchers find mental health prescription: Nature. (n.d.). Stanford University. https://news.stanford.edu/stories/2015/06/hiking-mental-health-063015

Stiglitz Report ec.europa.eu/eurostat/documents/8131721/8131772/Stiglitz-Sen-Fitoussi-Commission-report.pdf

SPI and ISEP Release Dataset Covering 10,000 Households and 2,000 Rural Enterprises | ISEP. (n.d.). https://sais-isep.org/news/spi-and-isep-release-dataset-covering-10000-households-and-2000-rural-enterprises/

United Nations University Return to Rural Communities: Resilience over Efficiency - Our World. (n.d.). https://ourworld.unu.edu/en/return-to-rural-communities-resilience-over-efficiency

WHO | What are integrated people-centred health services?

WHO | WHO consolidated guideline on self-care interventions for health: sexual and reproductive health and rights.

WHO | WHO core principles for achieving safe and sustainable management of health-care waste: Policy paper.

World Sustainable Development Forum (WSDF): www.worldsdf.org

World Wildlife Fund: Living Planet Report 2018 https://www.worldwildlife.org/publications/living-planet-report-2018

Annexure I

Extract of the annual address delivered by the President of the IAEE in Luxemburg on July 4-7, 1988 (available on the next page).

One area where our profession needs to make a much stronger entry than it has thus far is in the field of energy-environment interface issues. This becomes all the more important because the interface now covers a much wider expanse than was believed earlier. Not only are direct environmental effects of energy such as air and water pollution and acid rain serious enough to merit attention, but there is also now a definite basis for concern over the effects of energy use and production on the global climate. The greenhouse effect is no longer an abstract theory. Scientists have generated enough data to indicate that the carbon dioxide concentration in the world's atmosphere has increased from 275 PPMV in the pre-1850 period to 345 PPMV in 1985 (Ramanathan, 1988). Projections for the mid-twenty-first century indicate that this level will rise to between 400-600 PPMV by the year 2050. With some exceptions (see Ausubel and Nordhaus, 1983), few in the economics profession have looked at energy use and CO_2 projections, much less on the impact of these CO_2 projections on economic activity. It is beyond the capability, and certainly beyond the legitimate sphere of duty, of economists to look at physical or meteorological phenomena which link carbon dioxide levels with climatic change. Other disciplines and research capabilities in several parts of the world are actively investigating these happenings. But it is for energy economists to highlight long-run impacts of wide-spread and intensive combustion of fossil fuels on a range of economic activities. In doing so, some fresh conceptual models would need to be developed. But we can postpone a deeper interest in this subject only at the risk of a continuing insularity and myopia. Climate changes are already resulting in serious problems between the tropics, in the form of frequent droughts and floods, not the least cause for which is massive deforestation. The direct economic impacts of droughts and floods in the developing world are already substantial. Soil erosion in the Ganges basin in India, for instance, results in 6 billion tons of topsoil being washed away and dumped into the ocean annually. For India as a whole it is estimated that around 15 billion tons of soil erodes and washes into the Indian Ocean annually (Pachauri, 1987). If a market value was to be assigned to this quantity, we are perhaps losing topsoil of around $10 billion a year. This threatens the very measures of annual economic growth churned out by national income statistics, which would be dwarfed by the reduction in natural wealth taking place through such processes annually.

Annexure II

G lobal Warming of 1.5 °C an IPCC special report on the impacts of global warming of 1.5 °C above pre-industrial levels and related global greenhouse gas emission pathways, in the context of strengthening the global response to the threat of climate change, sustainable development, and efforts to eradicate poverty

Headline Statements

A. Understanding Global Warming of 1.5°C

A1. Human activities are estimated to have caused approximately 1.0°C of global warming above pre-industrial levels, with a likely range of 0.8°C to 1.2°C. Global warming is likely to reach 1.5°C between 2030 and 2052 if it continues to increase at the current rate (high confidence).

A.2. Warming from anthropogenic emissions from the pre-industrial period to the present will persist for centuries to millennia and will continue to cause further longterm changes in the climate system, such as sea level rise, with associated impacts (high confidence), but these emissions alone are unlikely to cause global warming of 1.5°C (medium confidence).

A3. Climate-related risks for natural and human systems are higher for global warming of 1.5°C than at present, but lower than at 2°C (high confidence). These risks depend on the magnitude and rate of warming, geographic location, levels of development and vulnerability, and on the choices and implementation of adaptation and mitigation options (high confidence).

B. Projected Climate Change, Potential Impacts and Associated Risks

B1. Climate models project robust differences in regional climate characteristics between present-day and global warming of 1.5°C and between 1.5°C and 2°C. These differences include increases in: mean temperature in most land and ocean regions (high confidence), hot extremes in most inhabited regions (high confidence), heavy precipitation in several regions (medium confidence), and the probability of drought and precipitation deficits in some regions (medium confidence).

B2. By 2100, global mean sea level rise is projected to be around 0.1 metre lower with global warming of 1.5°C compared to 2°C (medium confidence). Sea level will continue to rise well beyond 2100 (high confidence), and the magnitude and rate of this rise depends on future emission pathways. A slower rate of sea level rise enables greater opportunities for adaptation in the human and ecological systems of small islands, low-lying coastal areas, and deltas (medium confidence).

B3. On land, impacts on biodiversity and ecosystems, including species loss and extinction are projected to be lower at 1.5°C of global warming compared to 2°C. Limiting global warming to 1.5°C compared to 2°C is projected to lower the impacts on terrestrial, freshwater, and coastal ecosystems and to retain more of their services to humans (high confidence).

B4. Limiting global warming to 1.5°C compared to 2°C is projected to reduce increases in ocean temperature as well as associated increases in ocean acidity and decreases in ocean oxygen levels (high confidence). Consequently, limiting global
warming to 1.5°C is projected to reduce risks to marine biodiversity, fisheries, and ecosystems, and their functions and services to humans, as

illustrated by recent changes to Arctic sea ice and warm water coral reef ecosystems (high confidence).

B5. Climate-related risks to health, livelihoods, food security, water supply, human security, and economic growth are projected to increase with global warming of 1.5°C and increase further with 2°C.

B6. Most adaptation needs will be lower for global warming of 1.5°C compared to 2°C (high confidence). There are a wide range of adaptation options that can reduce the risks of climate change (high confidence). There are limits to adaptation and adaptive capacity for some human and natural systems at global warming of 1.5°C, with associated losses (medium confidence). The number and availability of adaptation options vary by sector (medium confidence).

C. Emission Pathways and System Transitions Consistent with 1.5°C Global Warming

C1. In model pathways with no or limited overshoot of 1.5°C, global net anthropogenic CO_2 emissions decline by about 45% from 2010 levels by 2030 (40– 60% interquartile range), reaching net zero around 2050 (2045–2055 interquartile range). For limiting global warming to below 2°C, CO_2 emissions are projected to decline by about 20% by 2030 in most pathways (10–30% interquartile range) and reach net zero around 2075 (2065–2080 interquartile range). Non-CO_2 emissions in pathways that limit global warming to 1.5°C show deep reductions that are similar to those in pathways limiting warming to 2°C (high confidence).

C2. Pathways limiting global warming to 1.5°C with no or limited overshoot would require rapid and far-reaching transitions in energy, land, urban and infrastructure (including transport and buildings), and industrial systems (high confidence). These systems transitions are unprecedented in terms of scale, but not necessarily in terms of speed, and imply deep emissions reductions in all sectors, a wide portfolio of mitigation options and a significant upscaling of investments in those options (medium confidence).

C3. All pathways that limit global warming to 1.5°C with limited or no overshoot project the use of carbon dioxide removal (CDR) on the order of 100–1,000 GtCO2 over the 21st century. CDR would be used to compensate for residual emissions and, in most cases, achieve net negative emissions to return global warming to 1.5°C following a peak (high confidence). CDR deployment of several hundreds of GtCO2 is subject to multiple feasibility and sustainability constraints (high confidence). Significant near-term emissions reductions and measures to lower energy and land demand can limit CDR deployment to a few hundred GtCO2 without reliance on bioenergy with carbon capture and storage (BECCS) (high confidence).

D. Strengthening the Global Response in the Context of Sustainable Development and Efforts to Eradicate Poverty

D1. Estimates of the global emissions outcome of current nationally stated mitigation ambitions as submitted under the Paris Agreement would lead to global greenhouse gas emissions in 2030 of 52–58 GtCO2eq yr-1 (medium confidence). Pathways
reflecting these ambitions would not limit global warming to 1.5°C, even if supplemented by very challenging increases in the scale and ambition of emissions reductions after 2030 (high confidence). Avoiding overshoot and reliance on future largescale deployment of carbon dioxide removal (CDR) can only be achieved if global CO2 emissions start to decline well before 2030 (high confidence).

D2. The avoided climate change impacts on sustainable development, eradication of poverty and reducing inequalities would be greater if global warming were limited to 1.5°C rather than 2°C, if mitigation and adaptation synergies are maximized while trade-offs are minimized (high confidence).

D3. Adaptation options specific to national contexts, if carefully selected together with enabling conditions, will have benefits for sustainable development and poverty reduction with global warming of 1.5°C, although trade-offs are possible (high confidence).

D4. Mitigation options consistent with 1.5°C pathways are associated with multiple synergies and trade-offs across the Sustainable Development Goals (SDGs). While the total number of possible synergies exceeds the number of trade-offs, their net effect will depend on the pace and magnitude of changes, the composition of the mitigation portfolio and the management of the transition (high confidence).

D5. Limiting the risks from global warming of 1.5°C in the context of sustainable development and poverty eradication implies system transitions that can be enabled by an increase of adaptation and mitigation investments, policy instruments, the acceleration of technological innovation and behavior changes (high confidence).

D6. Sustainable development supports, and often enables, the fundamental societal and systems transitions and transformations that help limit global warming to 1.5°C. Such changes facilitate the pursuit of climate-resilient development pathways that achieve ambitious mitigation and adaptation in conjunction with poverty eradication and efforts to reduce inequalities (high confidence).

D7. Strengthening the capacities for climate action of national and sub-national authorities, civil society, the private sector, Indigenous peoples, and local communities can support the implementation of ambitious actions implied by limiting global warming to 1.5°C (high confidence). International cooperation can provide an enabling environment for this to be achieved in all countries and for all people, in the context of sustainable development. International cooperation is a critical enabler for developing countries and vulnerable regions (high confidence).

Annexure III

Summary for policymakers of the global assessment report on biodiversity and ecosystem services of the Intergovernmental Science-Policy Platform on Biodiversity and Ecosystem Services

Some select Headline statements

A Nature and its vital contributions to people, which together embody biodiversity and ecosystem functions and services, are deteriorating worldwide.

A1 Nature is essential for human existence and good quality of life. Most of nature's contributions to people are not fully replaceable, and some are irreplaceable.

A2 Nature's contributions to people are often distributed unequally across space and time and among different segments of society. There are often trade-offs in the production and use of nature's contributions.

A3 Since 1970, trends in agricultural production, fish harvest, bioenergy production and harvest of materials have increased, but 14 of the 18 categories of contributions of nature that were assessed, mostly regulating and non-material contributions, have declined.

A4 Nature across most of the globe has now been significantly altered by multiple human drivers, with the great majority of indicators of ecosystems and biodiversity showing rapid decline.

A5 Human actions threaten more species with global extinction now than ever before

A6 Globally, local varieties and breeds of domesticated plants and animals are disappearing. This loss of diversity, including genetic diversity, poses a serious risk to global food security by undermining the resilience of many agricultural systems to threats such as pests, pathogens and climate change.

A7 Biological communities are becoming more similar to each other in both managed and unmanaged systems within and across regions.

A8 Human-induced changes are creating conditions for fast biological evolution - so rapid that its effects can be seen in only a few years or even more quickly. The consequences can be positive or negative for biodiversity and ecosystems, but can create uncertainty about the sustainability of species, ecosystem functions and the delivery of nature's contributions to people.

B. Direct and indirect drivers of change have accelerated during the past 50 years.

B4 In the past 50 years, the human population has doubled, the global economy has grown nearly fourfold and global trade has grown tenfold, together driving up the demand for energy and material.

B5 Economic incentives have generally favored expanding economic activity, and often environmental harm, over conservation or restoration. Incorporating the consideration of the multiple values of ecosystem functions and of nature's contribution to people into economic incentives has, in the economy, been shown to permit better ecological, economic and social outcomes.

B6 Nature managed by Indigenous peoples and local communities is under increasing pressure. Nature is generally declining less rapidly in Indigenous peoples' land than in other lands, but is nevertheless declining, as is the knowledge of how to manage it. At least a quarter of the global land area is traditionally owned, managed,3 used or occupied by Indigenous peoples.

C2 Nature is essential for achieving the Sustainable Development Goals. However, taking into consideration that the Sustainable Development Goals are integrated, indivisible, and nationally implemented, current negative trends in biodiversity and ecosystems will undermine progress towards 80 per cent (35 out of 44) of the assessed targets of Goals related to poverty, hunger, health, water, cities, climate, oceans and land (Sustainable Development Goals 1, 2, 3, 6, 11, 13, 14, and 15).

C3 Areas of the world projected to experience significant negative effects from global changes in climate, biodiversity, ecosystem functions and nature's contributions to people are also home to large concentrations of Indigenous peoples and many of the world's poorest communities.

D. Nature can be conserved, restored and used sustainably while other global societal goals are simultaneously met through urgent and concerted efforts fostering transformative change.

D3 Transformations towards sustainability are more likely when efforts are directed at the following key leverage points, where efforts yield exceptionally large effects (Figure SPM.9): (1) visions of a good life; (2) total consumption and waste; (3) values and action; (4)

inequalities; (5) justice and inclusion in conservation; (6) externalities and telecouplings; (7) technology, innovation and investment; and (8) education and knowledge generation and sharing.

3. Most of nature's contributions are not fully replaceable, yet some contributions of nature are irreplaceable.

4. Humanity is a dominant global influence on life on Earth, and has caused natural terrestrial, freshwater and marine ecosystems to decline.

6. The global rate of species extinction is already at least tens to hundreds of times higher than the average rate over the past 10 million years and is accelerating.

About the Author

Dr. R.K. Pachauri Former Chairman, Intergovernmental Panel on Climate Change (IPCC) 2002-2015

I. Early Life and Education

- Born on August 20, 1940, in Nainital, India.
- Education:
- Bachelor's degree in Mechanical Engineering from Indian Railways Institute of Mechanical and Electrical Engineering.
- Master's in Industrial Engineering from North Carolina State University (NCSU).
- Ph.D. in Industrial Engineering and Economics from NCSU.

II. Early Career

- Initial work with the Indian Railways.
- Research Associate at North Carolina State University.
- Assistant Professor at the University of West Virginia.

III. Leadership in The Energy and Resources Institute (TERI)

- Joined TERI in 1981.
- Served as Director-General of TERI from 1981 to 2016.
- Key Contributions:
- Transformed TERI into a global leader in research and policy on sustainable development.
- Expanded TERI's focus areas to include climate change, energy efficiency, renewable energy, and environmental sustainability.
- Established TERI University, which became a hub for advanced studies and research in sustainable development.

IV. Contributions to the Intergovernmental Panel on Climate Change (IPCC)

- Joined IPCC in 1995.
- Elected as Chairman of the IPCC in 2002, serving until 2015.

- Major Achievements:
- Led the IPCC during the Fourth Assessment Report (AR4) in 2007, significantly influencing global climate policy.
- Under his leadership, the IPCC was awarded the Nobel Peace Prize in 2007, which was shared with former U.S. Vice President Al Gore.
- Advocated for including climate change impacts on agriculture, health, and water resources in IPCC reports.

V. Advocacy and Public Engagement

- Prolific speaker and advocate for sustainable development and climate action.
- Instrumental in raising global awareness about the impacts of climate change.
- Participated in numerous international forums, including the United Nations Framework Convention on Climate Change (UNFCCC) conferences.
- Wrote extensively on energy, environment, and sustainable development issues.

VI. Academic and Advisory Roles

- Visiting professorships and lectureships at various prestigious universities worldwide.
- Served on the boards and advisory panels of numerous organizations, including:
- Yale University's Climate and Energy Institute.
- Asian Development Bank's Advisory Group on Climate Change.
- Advisor to the Indian government on energy and environmental policies.

VII. Awards and Honors

- The Government of India awarded him the Padma Bhushan (2001) and Padma Vibhushan (2008) for his contributions to science and engineering.

- Various international honors, including:
- The 'Officier De La Légion D'Honneur' by the Government of France in 2006.
- The 'Commander of the Order of Leopold II' by the King of Belgians in July 2009.
- The 'Commander of the Order of the White Rose of Finland' by the Prime Minister of Finland in February 2010,
- 'The Order of the Rising Sun, Gold and Silver Star' by His Majesty Akihito, Emperor of Japan in April 2010.
- The Mexican Order of the 'Aztec Eagle' by the President of Mexico in June, 2012.
- The Foundation Cassa di Risparmio di Mirandola conferred him with the Pico della Mirandola Prize in July 2013.
- More than twenty-five honorary doctorates from leading universities around the world.

VIII. Publications and Research

- Authored and co-authored numerous books, research papers, and energy, environment, and sustainable development articles.
- Extensive contributions to IPCC reports, including synthesis reports that summarize the state of knowledge on climate change.

IX. Legacy and Impact

- Visionary leader who integrated science, policy, and action to address global environmental challenges.
- Significant influence on global climate policy and sustainable development practices.
- Inspiring mentor and advocate for future generations of environmental leaders.

- The establishment of the POP Movement (www.thepopmovement.org) and the World Sustainable Development Forum or WSDF (www.worldsdf.org), among other initiatives, will continue his legacy of empowering youth and fostering global environmental stewardship.

Dr. R.K. Pachauri's professional accomplishments reflect his unwavering dedication to sustainable development and climate action. His visionary leadership at TERI and the IPCC, extensive advocacy, and public engagement have left an indelible mark on the global environmental landscape. His legacy inspires and drives efforts towards a more sustainable and resilient future.

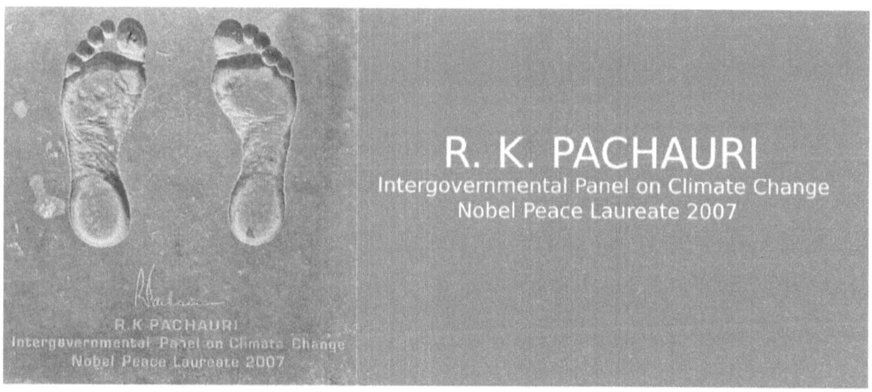

Read more about Dr. R.K. Pachauri at https://rkpachauri.org/